AF600149

THE COMPETENCE OF CHURCH AND STATE OVER MARRIAGE—DISPUTED POINTS

THE CATHOLIC UNIVERSITY OF AMERICA
CANON LAW STUDIES
No. 197

THE COMPETENCE OF CHURCH AND STATE OVER MARRIAGE —DISPUTED POINTS

BY

J. WILLIAM GOLDSMITH, B.C.S., S.T.L., J.C.L.
PRIEST OF THE DIOCESE OF CHARLESTON

A DISSERTATION

SUBMITTED TO THE FACULTY OF THE SCHOOL OF CANON LAW OF THE CATHOLIC UNIVERSITY OF AMERICA IN PARTIAL FULFILLMENT OF THE REQUIREMENTS FOR THE DEGREE OF DOCTOR OF CANON LAW

THE CATHOLIC UNIVERSITY OF AMERICA PRESS
WASHINGTON, D. C.
1944

NIHIL OBSTAT:
EDUARDUS ROELKER, S.T.D., J.C.D.
Censor Deputatus
Washingtonii, die 26 Aprilis, 1944.

IMPRIMATUR:
✠ EMMET M. WALSH, D.D.
Episcopus Carolopolitanus
Carolopoli, die 30 Aprilis, 1944.

COPYRIGHT, 1944, BY
THE CATHOLIC UNIVERSITY OF AMERICA PRESS, INC.

MURRAY & HEISTER—WASHINGTON, D. C.
PRINTED IN UNITED STATES

9

Christo
Regi Nostro
et
Genitrici
Virgini Immaculatae

TABLE OF CONTENTS

FOREWORD

The study of the competence of Church and State over marriage can be treated under various aspects. Because of the very practical nature of the question, each of these possible approaches to the subject has its own particular interest and importance. It would be of value to examine in detail the historical development of the problem: to follow the development of the Church's marriage legislation from a mere disciplinary control in the period of her infancy to a fully recognized jurisdiction in the Middle Ages; to show the inroads made upon that recognized competence by the post-Reformation resurgence of civil claims to authority over all marriages; and to study the difficulties confronting the Church in her attempt to assert and maintain her supernatural claims in regard to marriage. No less profitable would be a thorough doctrinal treatment of the subject, by establishing the dogmatic foundation of the present matrimonial discipline of the Church, by indicating the full scope of these dogmatic principles, and by drawing out their practical consequences.

Indeed, because of the intimate connection existing between these various phases of the question, the historical and the doctrinal elements will necessarily enter into the present study. The principal aim, however, will be to consider the problem of competence from the viewpoint of Public Ecclesiastical Law—to determine the exact nature and extent of the *rights* of Church and State over marriage, and by applying these rights to practical conflicts of jurisdiction to determine the proper and competent authority in such cases. Like Theology, Public Law has as its source Revelation; the matter, then, is the same, but the two sciences differ formally in their method of approach. They differ further in the fact that Public Law is a subordinate science which adopts the truths of Dogma as its principles—not by any means as gratuitous assumptions, but as theological conclusions.

The plan adopted for this present treatise will offer first a brief historical synopsis of the subject. The second chapter presents a summary of the fundamental juridical principles that necessarily govern the proper understanding and solution of the issues involved; the third chapter sets forth the dogmatic foundation of the juridical principles on marriage. The question of the relative competence of Church and State over marriage is not, for present purposes, the chief aspect of the problem, but chapter four treats this phase by way of further delineating the general principles that serve as a point of entry into the more specific problems under consideration. Thus properly orientated the present study deals primarily with the disputed points of the competence of Church and State over marriage—a competence which, though clearly established in the Code of Canon Law, yet presents practical difficulties in some of its functional aspects.

The writer wishes to extend a sincere expression of appreciation to His Excellency, the Most Reverend Emmet M. Walsh, Bishop of Charleston, for the opportunity to pursue graduate studies at the Catholic University of America, and to the members of the Faculty of the School of Canon Law for their kind direction and gracious assistance. Likewise, to all those cherished friends whose interest and help have been an inspiration and an encouragement to the completion of this work, the writer expresses his profound gratitude.

CHAPTER I

HISTORICAL CONSPECTUS

In order properly to understand the exact nature and source of the particular problems of competence that form the object of this study it is necessary to have at least a summary perspective of the historical background and development of the institute of competence in the law of the Church. But to trace in a thorough manner the full history and the entire jurisprudence on the subject would obviously be beyond the scope of the present investigation. To afford a properly balanced orientation, then, there will be presented a brief and concise summary of the general historical trend of competence over marriage, but into this will be introduced a detailed examination of the decretal material on the subject. The selection for special attention of this particular stage of development of the institute is not made arbitrarily; it is important because it presents a summation of the legislative and judicial trends of the preceding centuries and forms a basis for subsequent trends and developments. Moreover, the period of the decretals comes but shortly after the achieving of a goal with regard to the competence of the Church over marriage and but shortly before the emergence of the need to defend the position attained.

Article 1

Developments before the Time of the Decretals

It cannot be denied that in the first centuries of the Christian era the civil authority exercised extensive jurisdiction over marriage. But with the spread of Christianity through the Roman Empire, and particularly with the conversion of the emperors themselves, Christian principles gradually found their way into the imperial laws. This, however, wrought no essential change in the judicial systems, for matrimonial causes remained, as before, subject to the civil courts. And despite the fact that even in the early centuries of her existence the Church had some matrimonial legislation, nevertheless it was not recognized by the State. Although Constantine granted to the bishops some judicial power, yet this did not extend to the matter of divorces, for it must be remembered that divorce under Roman Law was *divortium ab intrinseco,* and there was no dissolution of a marriage by a judge. Under the converted Merovingian kings the authority of the bishops was somewhat further advanced. Hence in the Frankish kingdom the bishops were able to meet in provincial synods and enact canons, many of which dealt with Christian marriage; but their control over the faithful was disciplinary rather than legislative. The chief reason for the trend in that direction seems to lie in the relative weakness of the civil authority and the recognition on the part of the rulers that the Church was a strong force in maintaining order.

On the other hand, it must be remembered that it is of faith that Christ made marriage a sacrament.[1] Consequently, from the very beginning of her existence the Church must have had full jurisdiction over Christian marriage. However, the full realization of this dogmatic principle and its practical consequences were not evident from the beginning. One must bear in mind that in the early periods of her history the Church found a system of civil laws in possession and was able to establish her supernatural claims only gradually. Indeed, as one author has observed, " we cannot assign a precise date at which the Church commenced to exercise jurisdiction over matrimonial causes in her own name, and the civil authorities recognized that these matters lay outside the province of the secular tribunals. The change took place gradually, and was not effected by a formal grant . . . It began as a matter of custom, and gradually was recognized as a matter of right."[2] Esmein, however, is of the

[1] Conc. Trident., sess. xxiv, *de matrimonio,* prooemium, can. 1.

[2] Joyce, *Christian Marriage* (London: Sheed and Ward, 1933), pp. 223-224.

opinion that the process was complete by the close of the tenth century.[3]

Hence, during the first ten centuries of the Christian era, one finds the Church extending her jurisdiction over marriage from a mere disciplinary control to a recognized judicial and legislative competence. Paralleling this progress the Church moreover developed a certain jurisprudence of her own based on various ecclesiastical decrees. Some idea of the extent of this development may be gained from an examination of the laws on marriage that are to be found in the *Decretum Gratiani.* Gratian devoted ten Causes (nos. 27–36) in the second part of his *Decretum* to the legislation on marriage. The further progress of this legislation can be observed in Book IV of the Decretals of Gregory IX. This book contains not only the law on matrimony itself, but also the law on such closely related matters as espousals, dowry, legitimacy, separation from bed and board, etc.

The very existence of such far-reaching legislation has a probative value in establishing the competence and jurisdiction of the Church over matrimony, but the decretals must be examined to determine whether or not they set forth expressly the fact and the extent of this jurisdiction. Such an examination should reveal also the extent of the jurisdiction, if any, that had been retained by, or recognized in Church law as belonging to, the State.

Article 2

The Decretals and the Problem of Jurisdiction over Marriage

The first question to be considered in this study of the decretals may be stated in this manner: Is there in the decretals any express assertion of the right of the Church and of the extent of her jurisdiction over matrimony?

A careful study of the various papal decretals and of the conciliar materials contained in the collections of Gratian and of

[3] Esmein, *Le Mariage en Droit Canonique* (2. ed., 2 vols. [Vol. I rev. by R. Génestal, 1929, Vol. II rev. by R. Génestal & J. Dauvillier, 1935], Paris: Librairie de Recueil Sirey, 1929–1935), I, 27.

Gregory IX fails to reveal any such clear-cut statement of principle. Nowhere in them do we find a letter from any of the pontiffs or a decree of any of the councils that appears to have been elicited by some dispute between civil and ecclesiastical authorities regarding jurisdiction over marriage. The absence of any such document may perhaps have prompted the view already quoted, namely, that the change from civil to ecclesiastical jurisdiction was not brought about by a formal decree, but rather developed from custom to the status of a recognized right.

Viewed from the perspective of centuries it is not surprising that matters should have taken that course, for the very sacredness of marriage, even as a natural contract, would have tended to bring it within the sphere of the authority of the Church. Beyond that, the added dignity of its sacramental character when contracted between Christians would have urged the Church to press continually her inherent rights over marriage. That she actually did so is evident, as already observed, from the scope of her legislation on marriage. And that she did so without the need of a formal declaration is evident from the absence of such a formal assertion in her matrimonial jurisprudence.

To what, then, is to be attributed this trend? Apparently it arose from the recognition of the fact that things of a sacred nature, things pertaining to the divine, are in a category apart from things of the world; that by reason of their inherent diversity these two categories are subject to different authorities. Included in Gratian's *Decretum* is one letter that gives an indication of some recognition of that fact even as early as the close of the second century. The document is the first decretal of Pope Victor I (189–199), and it is concerned with the celebrated dispute over the Easter date. At the conclusion of his letter the Pontiff points to the fact that secular matters and divine matters lie within different spheres.[4] That this attitude towards the recognition of two spheres of authority existed also in the mind of the secular legislators may be illustrated by a statement found

---

[4] ". . . alia ratio est causarum saecularium, alia divinarum."—C. 22, D. III, *de cons.* Cf. also Jaffé, *Regesta Pontificium Romanorum* (2. ed., Leipzig, 1885–1888), n. 74.

in one of the constitutions of Justinian. There it is observed that the greatest gifts of God to man are the *sacerdotium* and the *imperium,* the one ministering to the divine, the other presiding over and directing human affairs.[5] It must be noted, however, that this did not prevent the emperors, and Justinian in particular, from claiming some jurisdiction in matters of the *sacerdotium.*

Article 3

The Decretals and the Problem of Jurisdiction over Matters Intimately Connected with Marriage

The fundamental reason, then, for the establishment of this right of jurisdiction on the part of the Church lies in the sacred character of marriage itself, and in the recognition on the part of the State that such matters were outside the scope of its authority. Of even more importance in the achievement of this goal was the fact that the sacraments were recognized as falling within the province of the Church. Moreover, since in the marriages of Christians the contract and the sacrament could not be separated, the Church quite logically pressed her claim to authority over matrimony in both of its aspects. On the other hand, the Church recognized that marriage has a necessary relation to circumstances of life which, though connected with marriage, pertain to the civil order. In regard to these purely civil effects the Church admits that the State has a determinate jurisdiction and competence.

In the decretals there are to be found certain border-line cases in which questions of the rights of inheritance, of hereditary succession, of dowry, and of legitimacy of birth are treated. Because these questions were usually intimately connected with marriage, there were times when the popes had to settle problems of jurisdiction—to define the extent of the competence of the Church, and to point out the limits of jurisdiction of the secular authority. A detailed study of such decretals as these will provide

[5] "Maxima quidem in hominibus sunt dona dei a superna collata clementia sacerdotium et imperium, illud quidem divinis ministrans, hoc autem humanis praesidens ac diligentiam exhibens; ex uno eodemque principio utraque procedentia humanam exornant vitam."—N. 6 (praefatio).

a better understanding of the questions and principles at issue in the particular problems that are to form the major object of the present study.

In the collection of Gregory IX there is contained a decretal of Pope Alexander III (1159–1181) addressed to Bartholomew, Bishop of Exeter, and to the Abbot of Hereford.[6] This letter, the exact date of which is unknown, is contained also in the *Compilatio Prima.*[7] It is concerned with a question of legitimate birth that had been brought before a secular judge in a claim for an inheritance. A certain R. had haled into court under the civil authority his cousin H. to obtain the share due to him from an inheritance left by their grandfather. H. objected to the claim of R. on the grounds that their grandfather had had two wives and that the father of the present R. was not born of a legitimate marriage; and for that reason H. maintained that R. could not vindicate his right of succession to a share in the inheritance. The question of legitimate birth was referred for decision to the Bishop of Norwich; but because of the long protracted delay in obtaining a decision from that prelate, the matter was eventually appealed to Rome.

Here it is of interest to note that Cardinal Hostiensis (Henry of Segusia) points out that it was proper that the parties should be sent to the Bishop of Norwich, because it pertains to the ecclesiastical curia, and not to the secular court, to judge the question of legitimacy connected with a person's birth.[8]

The Holy Father, wishing to avoid further delay, instructs Bishop Bartholomew to summon both parties before him and to hear the question in regard to the legitimacy of birth in the case, and to do so within two months. If within that time H. is unable to prove his objection to R.'s claim to the inheritance, the bishop is to return the case to the secular judge and to intimate

---

[6] C. 5, X, *qui filii sint legitimi,* IV, 17.

[7] *Comp. I,* IV, 18, 5. Cf. also Jaffé, *Regesta Pontificium Romanorum,* n. 14218.

[8] Hostiensis, *Lectura,* C. 5, X, *qui filii sint legitimi,* IV, 17, ad verbum *episcopo:* "(Episcopo) ad quem fuerunt partes missae quia ad ecclesiam, non ad saecularem curiam de hoc pertinet iudicare." See also the *Glossa ordinaria, loc. cit.,* ad verba *Quaestione nativitatis.*

to him that he should not overlook to hear and decide the suit for inheritance conformably to the question of legitimacy [which had been decided by the bishop himself].

The question of legitimate status at birth does not always lie outside the competence of the civil judge, for it may at times be a matter which is concerned with determining personal status. In fact, even among secular tribunals jurisdiction in this matter was at times conceded by Roman Law to a judge who ordinarily lacked jurisdiction over questions of juridical import as connected with birth. For instance, a judge, whose jurisdiction was limited to questions of property rights or inheritance rights, was recognized as also having the right to determine a question of status when it arose in such cases.[9]

Why, then, cannot the secular judge proceed in the case of R.? The reason is that in it there is a question affecting the person's status at birth, which status is dependent on the legitimacy of the marriage. The cause, therefore, is a purely spiritual one, and belongs principally to the Church to decide. Hence the civil judge cannot in such case either incidentally or in any other manner take cognizance of the question relating to status at birth.

(There are other decretals of Pope Alexander III that contain material relative to the general topic under consideration in this article; these, however, will not be treated at this point. There are among the decretals of other popes some in which there is reference to jurisdiction over questions of legitimacy. These latter will be examined first, and then the remaining decretals of Alexander III will be treated.)

In regard to the limitations upon the jurisdiction of the civil authority over questions affecting a person's origin and natal

---

[9] "Quotiens quaestio status bonorum disceptationi concurrit, nihil prohibet, quo magis apud eum quoque, qui alioquim super causa status cognoscere non possit, disceptatio terminetur."—C. (3.1) 3.

"Adite praesidem provinciae et ruptum esse testamentum Fabii Praesentis agnatione filii docete. Neque enim impedit notionem eius, quod status quaestio in cognitione vertitur, etsi super causa status cognoscere non possit: pertinet enim ad officium iudicis qui de hereditate cognoscit universam incidentem quaestionem quae in iudicium devocatur examinare, quoniam non de ea, sed de hereditate pronuntiat."—C. (3.8) 1.

status, both the *Glossa ordinaria* and the *Commentaria* of Cardinal Hostiensis refer to a decretal of Pope Honorius III (1216–1227), which is likewise contained in the collection of Gregory IX.[10] This letter, which was addressed to Louis VIII, King of France (1223–1226), was written from the Lateran on November 15, 1223.[11] Its contents concerned an asserted right of succession in the court among the nobility of Campania. One of the attendants of that court had died without issue, and the Queen of Cyprus had thereupon said that she, as next of kin to the deceased, ought to succeed to this place in the court. Someone, upon learning of this claim, went before the Pope and proposed that, since the queen had not been born of a legitimate marriage, she had no right of succession. The purpose of the Pope's letter to Louis was to warn the king that the question dealing with the status of her legitimacy of birth had been referred to the Holy See, and to ask him not to hear the question of succession until the question of legitimate birth had first been decided. Quite obviously, the main idea behind this monition and request was to avoid unnecessary complications and to maintain proper order in the judicial procedure. The decretal, however, has an important bearing on the present subject because of a statement that it contains, and more especially because of the commentaries provided on that statement by some of the glossators.

The Pope points out that the question concerning the legitimate natal status of the queen was referred to the Holy See for examination inasmuch as it was a cause which pertained to the ecclesiastical forum. Cardinal Hostiensis (+1271) gives as one of the reasons for this that to decide on a question of marriage belongs not to the representatives of man but to the vicar of God.[12]

[10] C. 3, X, *de ordine cognitionum,* II, 10. This decretal is also to be found in *Comp. V,* II, 5, 1.

[11] Cf. Potthast, *Regesta Pontificum Romanorum* (Berlin, 1874–1875), n. 7099.

[12] Hostiensis, *Lectura,* c. 3, X, *de ordine cognitionum,* II, 10, ad verba *Forum ecclesiasticum:* "Secunda [ratio] est, quia cum scriptum sit, quod Deus coniunxit, homo non separet, et per consequens pronunciare non fuisse matrimonium inter coniunctos non sit hominis sed solius Dei vicarii, ipse solus vicarius, et cui hoc committit, et non alius talem quaestionem examinare et diffinire potest."

Nicolaus de Tudeschis (Abbas Panormitanus) (1386–1453) uses much the same argument, but he develops it somewhat further. Besides stating the general rule that a secular judge can take cognizance of no spiritual cause either principally or incidentally, Panormitanus adds as a special reason for secular incompetence in this case the fact that matrimony is one of the seven sacraments of the Church.[13]

The *Glossa ordinaria* on the words "*ad forum ecclesiasticum*" of this same decretal merely makes the observation that a "cause concerning the status of a person's parentage pertains to the Church." But the gloss also refers to a letter of Pope Innocent III (1198–1216), written on December 30, 1205.[14] Towards the end of his letter, the pontiff directs the prelates to whom it is addressed to withhold themselves from the case in question unless it be a cause that is known to belong to the ecclesiastical judge.[15]

Of particular interest is the *Glossa ordinaria* on the words "*ecclesiasticum iudicem*" of this decretal of Innocent III. It states that among the causes which lie within the competence of the ecclesiastical judge are: matrimonial causes, questions of natal status, causes concerning the *ius patronatus,* disputes regarding tithes, and questions involving usury. In support of its assertion that matrimonial causes pertain to the Church, the gloss cites a

---

13 Panormitanus, *Commentarium,* c. 3, X, *de ordine cognitionum,* II, 10, n. 3: "Causa matrimonialis spectat ad iudicem ecclesiasticum non solum quando agitur inter ipsos coniuges et disputatur de validitate coniugii, sed etiam quando principaliter agitur de legitimitate filiorum cum decisio dependeat ex validitate matrimonii. Et est ratio secundum Innocentem quia cum scriptum sit: Quos Deus coniunxit, homo non separet, ita pronuntiare non fuisse matrimonium, vel esse inter aliquos, non homo sed solus vicarius Dei potest iudicare. . . . Hoc est ex illa ratione generali, quia iudex de nullo spirituali nec principaliter nec incidenter reconveniendo cognoscere potest. Item addo aliam rationem magis specialem: Matrimonium est unum de septem sacramentis ecclesiae. Merito non laicus sed ecclesia habet de eo iudicare. Item matrimonium fuit inductum de iure divino, et non civili, ideo ad vicarium ipsius instituentis, seu deputatum per eum pertinet cognitio eius, et non ad alium."

14 Potthast, *op. cit.,* n. 2645.

15 C. 11, X, *de foro competenti,* II, 2. This decretal may also be found in *Comp. III,* II, 2, 2.

decretal of Pope Alexander III.[16] The exact date of its writing is unknown.[17] At the end of his letter the Pope gives a definite qualification to this competence when he declares that matrimonial causes are to be treated not by just any judges whomsoever but by those who have the required jurisdiction and who are not ignorant of the provisions of the canons.[18] Quite obviously, these qualifications will exist only in the competent ecclesiastical authority.

Among the decretals of this same pope (Alexander III) is one that was addressed to the bishops of London and Worcester.[19] Like many other of the very numerous decretals of this pope, its date of composition is unknown.[20]

This letter is particularly interesting because in it Pope Alexander sets forth quite clearly that in a case involving both spiritual and temporal matters there is a definite line of demarcation between the jurisdictions of the ecclesiastical and the civil authorities; that, although the Church insists upon her right to judge those questions which fall within her competence, nevertheless she leaves entirely to the secular authority the civil rights and issues that may be in dispute.

The case was concerned with a dispute between a certain R. and a certain F., two noblemen, over some possessions. In the course of the litigation there had been interposed an objection that the mother of R. was of illegitimate birth. The Pope had previously committed this question to the bishops of London and Worcester for decision, but in doing so he had also inserted an instruction concerning the disposition of the disputed possessions. Apparently this interference with regard to the temporal issues involved in the dispute was resented by the king. Hence, in the

---

16 C. 1, X, *de consanguinitate et affinitate,* IV, 14. This letter is to be found also in the *Compilatio Prima,* IV, 14, 2.

17 Cf. Jaffé, *op. cit.,* n. 13838.

18 ". . . non sunt causae matrimonii tractandae per quoslibet, sed per iudices discretos qui potestatem habeant iudicandi, et statuta canonum non ignorent."

19 C. 7, X, *qui filii sint legitimi,* IV, 17. This decretal was likewise included in the *Compilatio Prima,* IV, 18, 4.

20 Jaffé, *op. cit.,* n. 13932.

present letter the Pope points out that he is mindful of the fact that the right to render judgment concerning such possessions belongs not to the Church but to the king. And lest he seem to detract from that right of the king (who has declared that rendering judgment in regard to these things belongs to himself), the Pope instructs the bishops to leave the decision about the disputed possessions to the king. But he insists that they are to take full cognizance of the principal cause, i.e., the question of legitimacy, and to render a decision on it.

The *Glossa ordinaria* on the words "*ad regem*" makes the observation that thus it is evident that spiritual and temporal jurisdiction are distinct and separate.[21]

Cardinal Hostiensis in his commentary on these same words of the decretal makes a similar observation. He adds that a secular judge may not interfere in spiritual things, nor may an ecclesiastical judge interfere in temporal matters.[22]

As an example of a decretal concerned with dowry and its relation to marriage, there is a letter of Pope Clement III (1187–1191).[23] Neither the names of the persons to whom it was directed nor the date of its writing are known.[24]

The Pope writes that one who is delegated to judge a matrimonial case should, if he grants a divorce or declares a marriage invalid, pronounce on the dowry to be restored, because the question of dowry is accessory to the principal cause.[25]

The *Glossa ordinaria* on the words "*incidens accessorie*" points out that this right and duty of pronouncing judgment concerning the dowry obtains only when the question of dowry is a cause

---

21 "Et sic patet quod iurisdictio spiritualis et temporalis distincta est et divisa."

22 Hostiensis, *Lectura*, c. 7, X, *qui filii sint legitimi*, IV, 17 ad verba *Nos attendentes:* "Et patet hic quod iurisdictio temporalis et spiritualis distincta est et divisa una ab alia, nec habet se intromittere saecularis de spiritualibus nec spiritualis iudex de saecularibus."

23 C. 3, X, *de donationibus inter virum et uxorem, et dote post divortium restituenda*, IV, 20. This decretal may be found also in *Comp. II*, IV, 14, 1.

24 Jaffé, *op. cit.*, n. 16589.

25 ". . . Quia igitur secundum iura vos, qui de matrimonio principaliter cognovistis, et de dote, quae est causa incidens, accessorie cognoscere valuistis et sententialiter diffinire . . ."

accessory to the matrimonial cause. For if during the marriage a suit regarding the dowry should arise because of some extrinsic reason, then the case would be subject to the civil authority.[26] It is of interest to note that the argument is based on the fundamental rule of law that the accessory follows the principal.[27]

From the brief analysis of the decretal material that has been presented, certain aspects of the problem of the competence of Church and State in relation to marriage are found to stand out quite clearly. In what have been termed the "border-line cases," i.e., cases involving a suit with regard to some matter more or less intimately connected with marriage, it is to be expected that there would have arisen a need to define the respective limits of jurisdiction of the ecclesiastical and the secular authorities. But even when such a need arose, it seems to have been called forth rather because of a failure in particular cases to distinguish the temporal and the spiritual issues involved than because of any deliberate attempt on the part of either authority to intrude itself into affairs that pertained to the other. For in each instance there was not so much an attempt to set up a new norm of procedure as there was an effort to interpret the immediate problem of competence in the light of certain well-established and recognized juridical principles.

This tendency appears to have been founded basically on the recognized and accepted doctrine of the establishment by God of two distinct authorities, the one to rule over things of a divine and spiritual nature, and the other to govern affairs of a secular and temporal character. And while the decretals which have here been examined do not treat *ex professo* of the question of the jurisdiction of Church and State over marriage (because jurisdictional issues were treated in decretals that were concerned with matters only indirectly connected with marriage), nevertheless they strongly intimate the existence within the competence

---

[26] "Bene dicit, accessorie, quia si non est matrimonium, neque dos. . . . Si vero constante matrimonio agat mulier de dote, quia forte maritus labitur facultatibus, vel dissipet bona sua, vel quia mortuus est: tunc causa illa agi debet coram iudice saeculari, quia modo causa dotis principalis est."

[27] "Accessorium naturam sequi congruit principalis."—Reg. 42, R. J., in VI°.

of the Church of a well-established authority over Christian marriage—and that because of its spiritual and sacred character. This fact is even more evident from the interpretations of the glossators and the commentators on the decretals.

And, finally, again it must be noted that the very existence and scope of the marriage legislation in the law of the Church at this medieval period gives a strong indication of the fact and extent of her jurisdiction over matrimony. This is particularly true in view of the pre-eminent position to which the Church had attained by the time of these decretals.

Article 4

Trends from the Time of the Decretals to the Present [28]

From the tenth to the fifteenth centuries the Church enjoyed to the full its native and proper power, legislative as well as judicial, over the marriages of Christians. This jurisdiction, which, as has already been noted, began as a matter of practice and custom,[29] had by the time of the historical period here in question come to be recognized in law. Gradually, however, this ideal condition was undermined. The first manifestation of infringement by the civil authority upon the rights of the Church was in the form of interference with the judicial power of the Church. Secular judges attempted to extend their sphere of competence from merely civil effects to matters involving the matrimonial bond itself. A little later this interference was carried over into the field of legislative competence. The beginnings were apparently harmless. The first intrusions were made only indirectly; matrimonial decrees (quite generally in conformity with the Church law) were enacted purportedly to " complete " the canonical legislation in certain respects.

The real impetus to civil usurpation of ecclesiastical authority over Christian marriage was given by the " Reformers " through their denial of the sacramental character of matrimony. Their erroneous views on the essential nature of Christian marriage

[28] For a more comprehensive history of this period, cf. Joyce, *Christian Marriage, passim;* and Esmein, *Le Mariage en Droit Canonique,* II, *passim.*

[29] Cf. *supra,* p. 2.

led them to place it under the control of the secular authority. They maintained that marriage is a purely secular contract, subject to the sole authority of the State, which is entirely competent to prescribe the form, to establish impediments, to dissolve the bond for certain causes in accordance with the natural and divine positive law. Protestantism brought with it many innovations; but in no respect was the divergence between the new and the old religion more complete than in regard to the doctrine on matrimony. It is quite to be expected that these developments should have brought forth a decisive declaration on the part of the Church. Hence, when the Council of Trent met, the errors of the Reformers in regard to marriage were thoroughly treated; and in the Tridentine legislation the Church declared and set forth in unequivocal terms her doctrine on marriage.[30]

But it was not easy to stem the mounting tide of opposition to these fundamental tenets of the Church on matrimony. The breach was further widened by the introduction of civil marriage. As the purely secular conception of the State gained acceptance, the State came to be upheld more and more as fully competent in its own right to regulate every phase of man's life. The complete secularization of marriage was effected during the French Revolution by the establishment of obligatory civil marriage. And while it does not exist everywhere in an obligatory form, yet the system of civil marriage in one form or another is found in most of the countries of the world today. Closely paralleling the rise of civil marriage has been the growth of civil divorce. Although it is true that divorce is not of its nature a logical consequence of the advent of civil marriage, yet the concept of a purely secular marriage, of a marriage stripped of all holiness, has tended to weaken the idea of the sacred and inviolable indissolubility of marriage. And from these two concepts—civil marriage and civil divorce—have arisen most of the pernicious evils that affect the social institution of marriage today.

Civil marriage in the strict or obligatory sense, i.e., imposed upon all indiscriminately in such a way that civil marriage alone

---

[30] Cf. Conc. Trident., sess. xxiv, *Doctrina de sacramento matrimonii; Canones de sacramento matrimonii; Decretum de reformatione matrimonii.*

is recognized as valid in the secular courts, does not exist in the United States. In this country the actual contracting of marriage through a civil ceremony is optional. However, the marriage laws of the several states are enacted for all, Christians and unbelievers alike. Out of this usurpation of the authority over Christian marriage that rightly belongs to the Church have come the conflicts and problems of competence that constitute the principal object of the present study.

CHAPTER II

JURIDICAL PRINCIPLES

ARTICLE 1

THE JURIDICAL CONCEPT OF SOCIETY

A. DEFINITION AND KINDS OF SOCIETY

1. Definition of Society:

In the juridical sense, society is an abiding union of men working together for a common good that is to be achieved by cooperative activity under a common authority; or, more briefly, a union of several men for the attainment of the same end by common means.[1] In this definition there are clearly set forth these elements: the material cause, which is a plurality of men; the formal cause, which is the juridical bond; the final cause, its purpose; and the efficient cause, the plurality of men together with the laws governing their activity. Of these elements necessary for the constitution of any society, the essential and fundamental element from a juridic standpoint is the end or purpose. For, according to the principle "*societates sunt ut fines,*" a society must be judged in the light of the end for which it was established. Not only does the end present the first reason for the being of a society, but also it gives the union its specific determination considered both in itself and in its juridical status.[2]

2. Kinds of Societies:

The bond which unites men in a group for the attainment of some end may be a purely ethical one; but in such a society there is no juridical obligation. In a juridical society, on the other

[1] Cavagnis, *Institutiones Iuris Publici Ecclesiastici* (4. ed., 3 vols., Romae, 1906), I, n. 38.

[2] Coronata, *Ius Publicum Ecclesiasticum* (2. ed., Taurini: Marietti, 1934), n. 16.

hand, there is a legal bond, a bond of law. When this bond is founded on a certain necessity imposed either by the natural law or by the divine positive law, men are no longer free to include or not include themselves in such a society. Thus, the State is a necessary juridical society by reason of man's nature as a social being. Likewise, the Church is a necessary society because it is established by divine law for the attainment of eternal life.[3]

By reason of the degree of their perfection, necessary juridical societies are classified either as perfect or as imperfect. A juridically imperfect society is one which has not in itself, either actually or virtually, all the means necessary to attain its own purposes and consequently must look to a superior authority to provide whatever means may be wanting. A juridically perfect society, on the other hand, is one which is self-sufficient and independent in its kind and has all the means, actual or virtual, at its command for a proper functioning to accomplish its end. It must be noted that this perfection is limited to that perfection which a society possesses in its own order; for, in the Providence of God, there is no *absolutely* perfect society. With man considered both in his nature and in his supernatural elevation, an absolutely perfect society would have to have as its end both the natural and the supernatural happiness of man.[4]

Of societies juridically and relatively perfect in their own order there are but two species: the State and the Church.[5] Each of these societies is supreme in its own order and completely autonomous, having the right to all those things (but only those things) that may be necessary or useful for the attainment of its

---

[3] Cappello, *Institutiones Iuris Publici Ecclesiastici* (2 vols., Taurinorum Augustae, 1907–1908), I, 17.

[4] Ottaviani, *Institutiones Iuris Publici Ecclesiastici* (2. ed., 2 vols., Civitate Vaticana: Typis Polyglottis Vaticanis, 1935–1936), I, n. 26.

[5] By the term *Church* is to be understood the One Universal Church, commonly defined by Catholic theologians as "coetus hominum viatorum eiusdem fidei christianae professione et eorumdem sacramentorum participatione adunatus, sub regimine legitimorum pastorum ac praecipue Romani Pontificis."—Tanquerey, *Synopsis Theologiae Dogmaticae* (23. ed., Parisiis: Desclée et Socii, 1930), I, n. 543.

relatively perfect and necessary end.[6] The supremacy of the juridically perfect society, like its perfection, is to be understood in a relative sense.[7] For, in the generic order, one perfect society is indirectly supreme over the other. This indirect supremacy of the one over the other flows not from a comparison of their natures, but from a consideration of their ends. And so the Church, possessing the higher end in a superior order, is indirectly supreme over the State.[8]

B. THE POWER AND FUNCTION OF PERFECT SOCIETIES

1. *The Relation of Origin and Power:*

If a society is formed in such a way that a new moral person is constituted and if it receives its power from without, then the measure of its power is determined by that of the original command.[9] The power of perfect societies is determined in this manner. For the power inherent in a perfect society is intimately bound up with the origin of that society in such a way that the necessary and proportionate power for the attainment of its end is established by the same law by which the perfect society was established. In brief, the juridic cause of a society is at the same time the juridic cause of its power.[10] And hence, if a perfect society has its origin in the natural law, its power likewise flows from the natural law; if it derives from the positive law, its power also emanates from that law. The Church, as has been observed, is a necessary perfect society which for its establishment is rooted in the divine positive law. Since, then, it has its origin through the direct command of God, the Church has also its

[6] Ottaviani, *op. cit.*, I, n. 33.

[7] Cavagnis, *op. cit.*, I, n. 60.

[8] Cf. Tarquini, *Institutiones Iuris Publici Ecclesiastici* (4. ed., Romae, 1865), n. 55; Wernz, *Ius Decretalium,* Vol. I, *Introductio in Ius Decretalium* (altera editio emendata et aucta, Romae, 1905), n. 10; Cavagnis, *op. cit.*, I, n. 404; Ottaviani, *op. cit.*, I, n. 26.

[9] The word *power* is used here to designate the concept of *auctoritas in se spectata* in contradistinction to the notion of *authority* in the sense of *auctoritas in subiecto*—a concept which is not of immediate concern in this context.

[10] Ottaviani, *op. cit.*, I, n. 29.

power from Him. The State, being likewise a perfect necessary society, is for its establishment grounded upon the natural law. Since, then, it derives its origin through that law, the State has likewise its power from God, i.e., from Him who is the author of the natural law.[11] And this, indeed, is altogether consonant with the Sovereignty of God, the Lord and Ruler of all; for "there is no power but from God." [12]

It is God who founded the Church, but it is men who give specific existence to the *form* in which the Society of the State actually manifests itself. In regard to the Church its Founder decreed as a necessity not only its existence but also its constitutional form of existence. In regard to the State God through the natural law decreed the necessity of its existence, but not the constitutional form of its existence. The latter determination was left to the free choice of mankind.

2. *The Function of Perfect Societies:*

Man has a twofold destiny. By the natural law he is ordained to a natural happiness; and by that same law he must seek his natural end in a social order. In other words, he naturally seeks social perfection—a perfection which he can attain only through society. Man has also a supernatural end in the order of grace to which he has been elevated and destined by God. This perfection, too, he must strive to attain through society. In the present economy, however, there is no society ordained to achieve the total perfection of man in both the natural and the supernatural order. For Almighty God has committed the work of man's perfection to two authorities. He has divided the care of the human race between the Church and the State, the one to provide for man's supernatural welfare, and the other to aid him in reaching his natural happiness.[13] To the Church in her capacity as man's guide to heaven has been assigned the threefold charge of teaching, ruling, and sanctifying.[14] Her power is primarily,

---

[11] Leo XIII, ep. encycl. *Immortale Dei,* 1 nov. 1885, §2—*Fontes,* n. 592.

[12] Romans, 13:1.

[13] Leo XIII, ep. encycl. *Immortale Dei,* §6—*Fontes,* n. 592.

[14] Matthew, 28:18–20.

though not exclusively, in the spiritual order. The State, on the contrary, has as its chief duty to safeguard the well-being of both the individual and the community in the temporal order. Its function in regard to things supernatural is purely ancillary inasmuch as its responsibility towards religion is to aid and protect, to favor and sanction.

The provinces of these two powers are distinct yet co-ordinate, divided yet complementary. The orderly connection that exists between them has been compared to the union of the soul and body in man. Moreover, the quality and scope of that connection is determined not only from the natures of each society, but also from the relative excellence and nobleness of their purposes. Whatever, therefore, in human affairs is of a sacred character, whatever pertains either of its own nature, or by reason of the end to which it is referred, to the salvation of souls or the worship of God, is subject to the power and judgment of the Church. But whatever falls within the compass of the civil and political order should properly be subject to the civil power.[15] This again is according to the divine command: "Render, therefore, to Caesar the things that are Caesar's, and to God the things that are God's." [16]

Article 2

The Juridical Relations of Church and State with Regard to "Res Mixtae"

In a general way the relations of the two species of perfect society have already been indicated. The indirect supremacy of the Church over the State by reason of the superiority of aim and purpose inherent in the former has been pointed out; a somewhat more specific indication of their relations has also been furnished in the treatment of their respective functions. Now there remains to be demonstrated the particular aspect of their juridical relations which is fundamental to the solution of the problems of competence that constitute the object of this study.

---

15 Leo XIII, ep. encycl. *Immortale Dei,* §6—*Fontes,* n. 592.

16 Luke, 20 : 25.

A. DEFINITION AND DIVISION OF "RES MIXTAE"

1. *Meaning and Extent of the Term:*

Things may be considered as being of a spiritual, temporal, or mixed character. This designation is to be understood not ontologically but *finaliter,* i.e., from a consideration of their inherent ends or acknowledged purposes. Thus, spiritual things are those which, although material in themselves, exclusively tend or are ordered to a supernatural end. Temporal things are those that, even though they be not material in themselves, are ordained to a temporal end.[17] Things of a mixed character (*res mixtae*) are those which are directly referred to a twofold end, scil., spiritual and temporal, and according to either respect are under the disposition of the competent society.[18] Hence there is a distinction between the notion of *res mixtae* (things of a mixed character which directly tend both to a spiritual and to a temporal end) and the notion of *res mixti fori* (issues which in their character are concurrently subject to an equal competence exercisable by the Church and the State alike). The former concerns the competence of both societies over the same matter but under different aspects. In that case Church and State are both interested in the matter, not in a cumulative but rather in a discrete manner. *Res mixti fori,* however, are those things in which Church and State have a cumulative power in such wise that whichever society takes up the matter first has the right to go through with it.

Res mixtae in the strict sense are those which of their very nature, by virtue of their natural quality and purpose, directly tend to both ends at the same time. In the broad sense, the concept of *res mixtae* includes those things which of themselves tend directly to only one end, but which through some added quality are ordered to the good of the other society also.[19]

2. *Classes of "Res Mixtae":*

A *res mixta* can be such either of its very nature or through a process which supernaturalizes its otherwise temporal character

[17] Coronata, *op. cit.,* n. 83.

[18] Ottaviani, *op. cit.,* II, n. 325.

[19] Ottaviani, *op. cit.,* II, n. 326.

or purely material content. The former (*res mixta naturalis*), while it remains within the limits of the order of nature, nevertheless is an object to which attaches a spiritual as well as a temporal import. Within this category, for example, would lie a marriage that is not endowed with the sacramental character. A *res mixta* which becomes such by being supernaturalized is one which by a positive act has been elevated to a higher order, to the supernatural order; such would be marriage raised to the dignity of a sacrament. A third class is sometimes distinguished as a *res mixta supernaturalis.* But a *res mixta supernaturalizata* and a *res mixta supernaturalis* are usually assimilated one to the other, for with regard to the question of competence they are both governed by the same juridic principles.[20]

Finally, there must be noted the two classes of effects possible to supernaturalized or supernatural matters of mixed character. Those effects which flow necessarily from the supernaturalized thing, and are so bound up with it that they can in no wise be disjoined therefrom, are called *inseparable.* Such inseparable effects cannot be made the subject of negotiation without at the same time having the substance of the thing to which they are annexed touched also. Two examples in point are the spiritual and supernatural graces and helps that necessarily proceed from Christian marriage, and the juridic condition of legitimated offspring. On the other hand, those effects which do not necessarily derive from the substance of a *res mixta* and are not unchangeably connected with it, but rather depend upon the command of positive law and therefore can be disjoined from the thing itself, are called *separable.* Moreover, when these separable effects are temporal, they are given the name of *merely civil effects.*[21]

B. THE JURIDICAL PRINCIPLES GOVERNING "RES MIXTAE"

Having in mind these concepts of the different kinds of *res mixtae,* and considering the notions of perfect societies as pre-

---

[20] Cf. Coronata, *op. cit.,* n. 87; Ottaviani, *op. cit.,* II, n. 327 and note 5; Cappello, *op. cit.,* I, 222.

[21] Ottaviani, *op. cit.,* II, n. 327.

viously set forth, one can establish certain definite juridical principles that must necessarily govern the power of such societies over matters that lie within the sphere of *res mixtae*. One may treat of these principles by attending first to the more general and then to the more particular divisions of matters or objects which are of a mixed character.

In the first place, *with regard to such matters, of whatever kind they be, civil society cannot make laws by prescinding from related ecclesiastical legislation; but it is the duty of the Church and the State to legislate by mutual agreement, safeguarding always the superior claims inherent in the Church as a society of a higher order.*[22]

This principle follows from the fact that according to the designs of God the two powers to which He has committed the care of the human race should work together in harmony and concord for the attainment of their respective ends.[23] The Church, it is true, has by reason of its existence as a society of a higher order the prevalent right in a question of *res mixtae*. But she has always recognized a certain duty of negative justice that binds her to give consideration to the prior and just legislation of the State, and not to hinder without necessity the operation of such laws. The State, on the other hand, has a corresponding obligation to respect the canonical legislation on such matters: not to prohibit what is prescribed by canon law; and not to impose on their mutual subjects what is forbidden by the Church.[24] If this duty to legislate by mutual agreement were faithfully attended to much difficulty would be avoided. But when these two societies function separately and enact laws that prescind one from the other, conflict of legislation can and does easily arise. And hence, in the event of conflict, the State, being the inferior society, must give way to the higher authority of the Church.

The second principle may be stated thus: *As regards both the*

---

[22] Cavagnis, *op. cit.*, I, n. 423; Cappello, *op. cit.*, I, 223; Ottaviani, *op. cit.*, II, n. 328.

[23] Leo XIII, ep. encycl. *Immortale Dei*, 1 nov. 1885, §6—*Fontes*, n. 592.

[24] Cavagnis, *op. cit.*, I, n. 424.

matters of a mixed character which are such of their very nature or essence, and also the effects which derive therefrom, each society can make laws that pertain to its own proper end.[25]

In these matters, then, each society may exercise its power over that aspect which pertains to its own proper end in the spiritual or in the temporal order, provided again that in case of conflict there be safeguarded the superior claims of the Church over the State. The first part of this proposition follows from the independence which each of these societies enjoys; and the proviso is a corollary of the indirect superiority that the Church has been demonstrated to have over the State.

From this principle it is evident that a thing which of its nature is of a mixed character, even though it tend directly unto a spiritual end, does not by that fact lose its place in the order of nature as a thing ordained to a temporal end also. Hence the fact that instruction given to children in schools (especially to those in elementary schools) should concern also their spiritual welfare, does not withdraw the school from its place in the temporal order. On the contrary, the school must still fulfill in that order its task of providing the civic education of youth.[26] Since education is essentially a social and not a merely individual activity, and since it should strive for the perfection of the whole man in the order of nature and in the order of grace, the concern for achieving the purpose of education belongs consequently to both of these societies in due proportion. Thus, the State would have direct control over the temporal aspects of education; and the Church, direct control over the spiritual. But again by reason of her indirect superiority, the Church's power includes indirectly the temporal aspects that may be necessary for the attainment of her aims; hence she may control also the physical and civil factors in education as well as the religious and moral. The State, on the other hand, within the proper limits of its own order can control indirectly the curriculum in church schools by, for example, standardizing certain educational requirements. Another

---

[25] Cavagnis, *op. cit.*, I, n. 426; Cappello, *op. cit.*, I, 225; Ottaviani, *op. cit.*, II, n. 329.

[26] Ottaviani, *op. cit.*, II, n. 329.

example of a matter which of its very nature is of a mixed character may be found in a marriage that has no sacramental character, as, e.g., in a marriage between two unbaptized persons. Prescinding from the question as to whether the rights over such a marriage belong to the State *ex iure proprio et nativo* or only *ex iure devolutivo et hypothetico,* one must admit that the State is recognized to have certain rights over such a marriage; but her rights therein are by no means exclusive, for marriage even as a natural contract has a sacred character. Indeed, radically and fundamentally it is that very sacredness that places the power to dissolve the bond of marriage outside the competence of the State.

A third principle governing *res mixtae* concerns those that are either supernatural or supernaturalized. *The civil power can make no disposition with respect either to the substance or to the inseparable effects of supernatural or supernaturalized "res mixtae"; but the power of the State extends only to the merely civil (i.e., separable and temporal) effects of these things, the while it must preserve the proper subordination to the ecclesiastical law.*[27]

The reason for this is that such things are in and of themselves spiritual; this spiritual quality belongs to them either of themselves as supernatural things, or by their elevation to a higher order whereby they have become endowed with the nature of supernatural things. It is, therefore, only incidental that they have some temporal effects; and, consequently, it is only in a broad sense that they may be called matters of a mixed character. Since the Church alone has competence over things essentially supernatural, it is evident that she alone has full power over the substance of things that are supernatural or supernaturalized. The same is true in regard to the inseparable effects of these things, for, as has already been shown, such effects are intimately connected with the substance and follow its nature according to the principle *accessorium sequitur principale.* And, therefore, to that power which is competent to take cognizance of and to

---

[27] Cavagnis, *op. cit.,* I, nn. 428–432; Cappello, *op. cit.,* I, 225–229; Coronata, *op. cit.,* n. 87; Ottaviani, *op. cit.,* II, n. 330.

make regulations concerning the cause, it belongs also to dispose of such effects as are necessarily connected with the same cause.[28]

Concerning the merely civil effects, the State, it has been noted, can legislate provided that these civil regulations be not opposed to the laws of the Church. It is obvious from the definition of separable temporal effects that they are directed to the end which is proper to civil society; moreover, they do not derive from the substance of the thing and are not inseparably linked to it. Consequently, by nature they fall within the sphere of the temporal order and are subject to the power of the State. That competence over these temporal effects must, however, be exercised with moderation and with due regard for the spiritual substance from which they flow and over which the Church has full power. If, therefore, an unjust law is enacted by the State in such matters the Church can exempt her subjects from that law; and even if the law be useful from the viewpoint of civil society but is in any way harmful to the spiritual good, the Church again can exempt her subjects from its observance.

As an example of a supernatural *res mixta* one can point to baptism; by reason of its divine institution as a sacrament it lies outside the competence of the civil power which exists within the temporal order, and which, accordingly, cannot exercise its jurisdiction over a thing in the spiritual order. The State, then, could never settle the question of the validity or invalidity of the administration of baptism; but if a question of inheritance turned upon the baptism of some individual, the State could decide a point of bare fact as to whether baptism as a ceremony had or had not been administered to that individual.

The contract of marriage through its elevation by Christ to the dignity of a sacrament is in the class of supernaturalized *res mixtae*. Its substance is supernaturalized and consequently is wholly subject to the power of the Church. From such a marriage there flow certain effects which have an intrinsic and neccessary connection with the substance of the thing, and are inseparable from it. Such effects are, for example, questions concerning the freedom of the parties to contract marriage, the

[28] Ottaviani, *op. cit.*, II, n. 330.

unity and indissolubility of the marriage bond, the legitimacy of offspring, etc. And, as previously pointed out, concerning these effects the Church alone is competent to make laws and to pass judgment. There are other effects that are connected only incidentally with the substance of the matrimonial contract, and are, in consequence, separable from it. Among such effects are the rights of succession in regard to nobility or in regard to property, the rights to share in an inheritance, dowry rights, etc. The State can make laws establishing certain conditions to be fulfilled in order that these effects may follow legally—provided, as always, that these conditions are not contrary to divine or ecclesiastical law.

In all questions concerning *res mixtae,* then, there should be preserved the fundamental competence of Church and State, each in its own proper order; and in the event of conflict the indirect superiority of the Church must, because of its higher aims, prevail. In conclusion, it may well be noted that the tendency of the Church has been clearly indicated by her insistent and repeated pleas for the maintenance of that harmonious union which should characterize the relations of the spiritual and the temporal authorities. For, as Pope Leo XIII has observed: ". . . in such arrangement and harmony is found not only the best line of action for each power, but also the most opportune and efficacious method of helping men in all that pertains to their life here, and to their hope of salvation hereafter." [29]

---

[29] Ep. encycl. *Arcanum Divinae,* 10 feb. 1880, §22—*Fonte,* n. 580; English translation from *The Pope and the People* (London: Catholic Truth Society, 1937), p. 40.

CHAPTER III

THE CATHOLIC DOCTRINE ON MARRIAGE—ITS SACRED CHARACTER

In the foreword to this study it was pointed out that the nexus between the juridical and the doctrinal aspects of the problem to be treated is necessarily an intimate one. The juridical principles upon which the whole treatise is based have been presented in the preceding chapter. It will be the burden of this present chapter to set forth briefly the dogmatic and moral principles that are fundamental to the subject under consideration.

In treating the Catholic doctrine on marriage theologians distinguish between marriage as a natural institution and marriage as a supernatural entity or as a sacrament. These same divisions will be followed here. Accordingly, in the first article marriage as a natural institution will be examined—first as a contract and then as a permanent state; in the second article the Catholic teaching on marriage as a sacrament will be presented.

Article 1

Marriage as a Natural Institution

As a contract of the natural order marriage is a bilateral agreement between one man and one woman whereby is given and accepted the exclusive and perpetual right both to those mutual bodily functions which of their nature serve the purpose of the begetting of offspring, and to the other normal elements of common conjugal life.[1] The formal cause of this contract is the free and mutual consent externally manifested by the contracting parties. And although the material cause is the reciprocal transfer of bodily rights for the performance of the marital act, yet the

[1] Cf. Tanquerey, *De Poenitentia et Matrimonio, Pars Dogmatica* (4. ed., Parisiis: Desclée et Socii, 1930), n. 884.

contract is a consensual rather than a real one. The contract is, therefore, essentially constituted by the mere consent and does not require to be supplemented by carnal intercourse for its completion.[2]

To give rise to a true matrimonial contract this consent must be given freely,[3] simultaneously, and reciprocally, and must be manifested externally by two persons capable of contracting marriage. This implies that the individuals be both rationally and physically fit to enter marriage; and further, for the licitness of the contract that the parties be free of all impediments, and for validity that they be free of all diriment impediments. The rational fitness requires not only that the parties be capable of a human act and have at least a virtual intention of contracting marriage, but also that they have at least a general notion of the manner in which conjugal rights are exercised. The physical fitness demanded is a capacity for true sexual intercourse.

Of itself the contract thus entered into is lawful and valid when it is conformed to the natural and divine positive law, but other requisites for the lawfulness and the validity of the contract may be further determined by ecclesiastical law for Christian marriages and by civil law for the marriages of unbelievers. It is a corollary of these elements of lawfulness and validity that all men may contract marriage unless by law they are forbidden to do so.[4]

Now, the matrimonial contract itself is a mere transitory act, but as such it is the efficient cause of the solemn marriage bond which in the moral order is the sacred and inviolable foundation

---

[2] Cf. Saint Thomas, *Summa Theologica, Suppl.*, q. 45, a. 1; Tanquerey, *De Poenitentia et Matrimonio*, n. 900; Davis, *Moral and Pastoral Theology* (2. ed., 4 vols., New York: Sheed & Ward, 1936), IV, 177. Cf. also canon 1081.

[3] "This freedom, however, regards only the question whether the contracting parties really wish to enter upon matrimony or to marry this particular person . . ."—Pius XI, ep. encycl., *Casti Connubii*, 31 dec. 1930—*AAS*, XXII (1930), 539–592. Cf., in particular, p. 541, for the doctrine here quoted.

[4] Wernz-Vidal, *Ius Canonicum*, Tomus V, *Ius Matrimoniale* (7 vols. in 8, Romae: apud Aedes Universitatis Gregorianae, 1925), n. 145 and note 1; cf. canon 1035.

of that permanent union of conjugal life lived in common by two persons as husband and wife.[5] This unity of body, of mind, and of heart, to which the parties dedicate themselves, is the essence of every marriage from the beginning of time.

It has been observed that the essence of the contract consists in that act of deliberate will by which each party transfers and accepts rights; but these rights are exchanged in view of the ends of marriage that are to be attained in the permanent state of marital life. The ends of marriage are distinguished by theologians as primary and secondary.

The primary and essential end of matrimony is the procreation and education of children.[6] This is an obvious postulate of nature, as may be inferred not only from the physical differences in sex of the contracting parties with the consequent strong inclination to bodily union, but also from the origin of marriage in the natural law as the means of propagating the species and from the divine command which bade man and woman to increase and multiply.[7]

For man the propagation of the species has a far deeper significance than it has among any other creatures. It is for that reason that the education of children is so intimately bound up with their procreation that the two unitedly constitute the primary end of marriage. Every human being possesses a spiritual and immortal soul, created directly by God and destined to everlasting happiness in His heavenly kingdom. When, therefore, married persons generate a human body into which Almighty God infuses an immortal soul made to His own image and likeness, they co-operate intimately with the Creator in providing another heir to the kingdom of heaven. Aside, then, from the natural assistance and protection that born offspring require of their parents, there is demanded the perfection of the human being through education—intellectual, religious, moral, and physi-

[5] Cf. Wernz, *Ius Decretalium*, Vol. IV, *Ius Matrimoniale* (Romae, 1904), n. 28.

[6] Cf. Tanquerey, *De Poenitentia et Matrimonio*, n. 887; Merkelbach, *Summa Theologiae Moralis* (editio altera aucta et emendata, 3 vols., Parisiis: Desclée, 1935–1936), III, n. 769; canon 1013, §1.

[7] Genesis, 1:28.

cal—an education befitting his exalted destiny and calculated to guide him to the ultimate end of all human life, God Himself.

The secondary end of marriage is the mutual help and comfort of the spouses and the allaying of concupiscence.[8] The marital union is intended to provide the parties with happiness and contentment. This secondary objective of marriage flows naturally from the primary end. United in their efforts to care for and rear the children begotten of their mutual love, the spouses lean upon each other for sympathetic understanding, for whole-hearted affection, for devoted assistance and comfort in the necessities and trials of life. Marriage, moreover, affords the means of allaying, or of providing a lawful outlet for, the strong inclination to sexual gratification that is normally found in every human being.

When these ends or objectives of marriage are considered in a cumulative manner and in all their relations, there flow from them certain essential properties or characteristics of the matrimonial bond. These essential properties of marriage are two, namely unity and indissolubility.[9] The unity of marriage arises from the fact that the conjugal union is entered into between one man and one woman, each having marital rights and duties with respect to the other, to the exclusion of all other persons. Opposed to this quality of unity is simultaneous polygamy, which may be either polyandry (the union of one woman with several husbands) or polygyny (the union of one man with several wives). It is evident that simultaneous polygamy is in a general way opposed to the natural law in that it is subversive of the mutual love, the self-consecration of each spouse to the other, and the domestic peace and happiness that should characterize the marital relationship. More specifically, simultaneously polyandry is contrary to the primary precepts of the natural law, for it effectively excludes the attainment of the primary purpose of marriage; simultaneous polygyny is opposed to the secondary precepts of the natural law, for though it may not destroy the

[8] Cf. Tanquerey, *De Poenitentia et Matrimonio,* n. 888; Merkelbach, *Summa Theologiae Moralis,* III, n. 769; canon 1013, §1.

[9] Merkelbach, *Summa Theologiae Moralis,* III, n. 809; Leo XIII, ep. encycl. *Arcanum Divinae,* 10 feb., 1880, §4—*Fontes,* n. 580; canon 1013, §2.

essential economy of marriage with respect to the primary end, it is nevertheless generally harmful to the attainment of that end and even more directly militates against the secondary objective of marriage.[10] Although under the Old Covenant polygyny was permitted by God, nevertheless Christ our Lord explicitly recalled marriage to its original unity; hence under the New Covenant simultaneous polygamy is forbidden by divine positive law.[11] According to the common teaching of theologians and according to decisions of the Church, this law of monogamy is binding on all mankind, Christians and unbelievers alike.[12]

The other essential property of matrimony is its indissolubility. The marital bond is possessed of an absolute intrinsic indissolubility, for any attempt by the parties to dissolve their own marriage by their own will and private authority is contrary to the primary precepts of the natural law.[13] The reason adduced for this principle is that an intrinsic dissolubility is directly opposed to the primary purpose of marriage.[14] Since, however, the primary end of marriage would not be fundamentally impeded if marriage were dissoluble after children were born and educated, *absolute extrinsic* indissolubility is not by the natural law an indispensable quality of the marital bond.[15]

Yet it is evident that even extrinsic dissolubility is opposed to the secondary objective of marriage and renders difficult the at-

[10] For a more detailed exposition and explanation of these principles, cf. Merkelbach, *Summa Theologiae Moralis,* III, n. 811; De Smet, *Betrothment and Marriage* (2. ed., trans. from the 3rd Latin edition of 1920 by W. Dobell, 2 vols., Brugis: Charles Beyaert, 1923), nn. 303-304. Cf. also Saint Thomas, *Suppl.,* q. 65, a. 1.

[11] Matthew, 19:3-8; cf. also Conc. Trident., sess., xxiv, *de matrimonio,* can. 2.

[12] Cf. Merkelbach, *Summa Theologiae Moralis,* III, n. 814; Cappello, *Tractatus Canonico-Moralis de Sacramentis,* Vol. III, *De Matrimonio* (ed. quarta emendata et aucta, Romae: Marietti, 1939), n. 43.

[13] Merkelbach, *Summa Theologiae Moralis,* III, n. 816; Cappello, *De Sacramentis,* III, n. 45. Cf. also Wernz, *Ius Matrimoniale,* n. 51.

[14] Saint Thomas, *Suppl.,* q. 67, a. 1, ad 4; *Contra Gentiles,* III, n. 123.

[15] It must be borne in mind that there is question here of marriage as a natural institution. The quality of absolute intrinsic and extrinsic indissolubility that is peculiar to a ratified and consummated Christian marriage will be considered in the next article of this chapter.

tainment of the primary objective. Hence, marriage is endowed with a relative extrinsic indissolubility by the secondary precepts of the natural law. It is relative in the sense that a limited and restricted dissolubility is possible under certain conditions determined by the divine law and only under divine authority.[16] These principles of indissolubility are determined not alone by the natural law, but also by the divine positive law, both in the decree of the original institution of marriage and in the command of Christ.[17]

Basic to the teaching of theologians and the doctrine of the Church on all these points is the recognition of and the insistence upon the sacred character of marriage even as a natural institution. The peculiar sanctity of marriage flows directly from its origin and indirectly from its purposes and its nature. Matrimony was not instituted by the will of man or by any human authority, but from the very beginning by the authority and command of God. And from its very inception the Creator signed and sealed, as it were, the marital union of man and woman with a sacred unity and perpetuity, that it might the more fittingly serve the designs of His Providence as an instrument of the divine Omnipotence to bring forth and rear in His service children destined to the eternal joys and happiness of heaven. On this point, Pope Leo XIII says: " Marriage has God for its author, and was from the beginning a kind of foreshadowing of the Incarnation of His Son; and therefore there abides in it a something holy and religious; not extraneous, but innate; not derived from men, but implanted by nature." [18]

Enlarging upon this same point, Pope Pius XI says: " Even by the light of reason alone and particularly if the ancient records of history are investigated, if the unwavering popular conscience is interrogated and the manners and institutions of all races examined, it is sufficiently obvious that there is a certain sacredness and religious character attaching even to the purely natural

---

[16] Cf. Tanquerey, *De Poenitentia et Matrimonio,* nn. 913–919; Merkelbach, *Summa Theologiae Moralis,* III, n. 816; Cappello, *De Sacramentis,* III, n. 45; Wernz, *Ius Matrimoniale,* nn. 697–698.

[17] Genesis, 2: 24; Matthew, 19: 3–8.

[18] Ep. encycl. *Arcanum Divinae,* 10 feb. 1880, §11—*Fontes,* n. 580; *The Pope and the People,* p. 31.

union of man and woman . . . This sacredness of marriage which is intimately connected with religion and all that is holy arises from the divine origin . . . , from its purpose which is the begetting and educating of children for God, and the binding of man and wife to God through Christian love and mutual support; and finally, it arises from the very nature of wedlock, whose institution is to be sought for in the farseeing Providence of God, whereby it is the means of transmitting life, thus making the parents the ministers, as it were, of the divine Omnipotence." [19]

Article 2

Marriage as a Sacrament

It is an article of faith that the matrimonial contract between two baptized persons is a sacrament of the New Law.[20]

Exactly when Christ made marriage a sacrament is not known; this He may have done at the marriage feast of Cana or when He restored to marriage its original unity and indissolubility, but the best view seems to be that He did so in the course of the forty days between His resurrection and His ascension. That Christ our Lord did elevate Christian marriage to the dignity of a sacrament is demonstrated by theologians from the implications of Sacred Scripture, from the writings of the Fathers, and from the teaching of the Church.[21]

The sacramental character of matrimony is shown also from the fact that, in common with all the sacraments, it has all the requisite and essential notes of a sacrament: it was instituted by Christ; it signifies and is capable of conferring grace; it is essentially constituted by matter and form; it is an external and sensible sign. The matter of this sacrament is the signs or words by which there is effected a mutual transfer of rights on the part of

---

[19] Ep. encycl. *Casti Connubii—AAS,* XXII (1930), 570; English translation from *Selected Papal Encyclicals 1896 to 1931,* Vol. I (London: Catholic Truth Society, 1939), 39.

[20] Conc. Trident., sess. vii, *de sacramentis in genere,* can. 1; sess. xxiv, *de matrimonio,* prooemium, can. 1. Cf. also canon 1012, §1.

[21] Cf. Tanquerey, *De Poenitentia et Matrimonio,* nn. 948–949 and 952–956; Merkelbach, *Summa Theologiae Moralis,* III, n. 780.

each spouse over the body of the other; the form is the mutual and exteriorly manifested acceptance of these mutually transferred rights; and the ministers of the sacrament of matrimony are the contracting parties themselves.[22]

Finally, theologians generally present an argument of reason derived from a consideration of the fitness of such a sacramental elevation as regards matrimony. Commenting on this fitness of the elevation of marriage to the dignity of a sacrament, Farrell says: " [Marriage] came directly from the hands of God with the nature of man; from the beginning it had something of the divine about it. When God sent His only Son that men might have life more abundantly, it was inevitable that greater fullness, holiness, greater union would be given to this climax of that heroic thing which is human love. But only God could have thought of making it a sacrament; a source of divine as well as of human life." [23]

It is important, however, to note that the sacrament of matrimony is not something that is superadded to the natural contract of marriage; rather it is identical with it. Hence in Christian marriage the contract is inseparable from the sacrament, and " for this reason, the contract cannot be true and legitimate without being a sacrament as well." [24]

All that has been said in the preceding article on marriage as a natural institution holds true with an even deeper significance for the sacrament of matrimony. By virtue of its sacramental dignity, Christian marriage has a higher and nobler purpose than was previously given to the purely natural union. Besides the propagation of the human race, it looks to the begetting of children for the Church of Christ and to the educating of these children in the bosom of that Church as servants and worshippers of the true God through His Only-Begotten Son. The fact that Christian marriage is a sacred sign or symbol of the intimate bond

---

[22] Cf. De Smet, *Betrothment and Marriage,* nn. 181–182.

[23] Farrell, *A Companion to the Summa* (4 vols., New York: Sheed and Ward, 1939–1942), IV (*The Way of Life,* 1942), 404.

[24] Leo XIII, ep. encycl. *Arcanum Divinae,* 10 feb. 1880, §12—*Fontes,* n. 580. Cf. also canon 1012, §2.

which unites Christ and His Church [25] is indicative of the special effects, the sacramental graces, that come to the spouses through this sacrament—abundant supernatural helps to a conjugal life of generosity and love, making of their common life a means of a deeper, fuller participation in the life of God.

Likewise, the two essential properties of marriage, namely its unity and indissolubility, which even in the natural contract of marriage are holy and inviolable, receive in the sacrament a special quality of sanctity and firmness and strength. Indeed, the only type of marriage that is endowed with an *absolute* intrinsic and extrinsic indissolubility, so that it can be dissolved only by the death of one of the parties, is a consummated sacramental marriage.[26] In such a marriage, although the bond is certainly stronger, nevertheless there does not seem to be in its nature any reason on account of which it could not be dissolved by divine authority. But, in fact, God has communicated to the Church no power to dissolve a marriage that is ratified and consummated; hence, its particular indissolubility derives directly from the positive divine will, and more remotely from the accidental perfection which such a marriage possesses by virtue of its sacramental nature together with the fact of its consummation.[27]

---

[25] Cf. Leo XIII, ep. encycl. *Arcanum Divinae,* §12—*Fontes,* n. 580; Pius XI, ep. encycl. *Casti Connubii—AAS,* XXII (1930), 552.

[26] "Undoubtedly legitimate marriage (consummated or not consummated) is not dissoluble *as long as both parties remain unbelievers;* still this does not proceed from the natural firmness of the bond, nor by strict law from a defect of the Church's power, but from the defect of the subjection of marriage to the power of the Church, to which alone belongs, to the exclusion of the civil authority, the divine power of dissolving matrimony; however there is no absolute indissolubility, but a dissolubility relative to the subsisting state of infidelity on either side."—De Smet, *Betrothment and Marriage,* I, 251, note 1.

[27] Cf. especially De Smet, *Betrothment and Marriage,* nn. 356 and 367. See also Merkelbach, *Summa Theologiae Moralis,* III, n. 818; Cappello, *De Sacramentis,* III, n. 755; canon 1118.

CHAPTER IV

THE RELATIVE COMPETENCE OF CHURCH AND STATE OVER MARRIAGE

Since marriage is an institution not only of the natural law but also of the divine positive law, it is regulated principally by the laws given by God. But it is not sufficient to say simply that marriage is subject to the law of God, for the inability of men to understand fully all the implications of the divine precepts makes it necessary that there be some further application and determination of these principles. This further specification of the divine law must, in accordance with the dispositions of God's Providence, be made by some legitimate human authority. Now, marriage is destined through its institution to subserve various beneficial interests: the private good of the contracting parties, the good of the family, and the public good of civil society as well as that of the Church. Hence, as Saint Thomas says, marriage is subject to diverse authorities.[1] It remains then to consider under what aspects marriage is to be regulated by the law of the Church and to what extent it is to be governed by the law of the State.

Article 1

The Competent Authority over the Marriages between Baptized Persons

Since marriage as an institution is intimately bound up with the public good of society and must be regulated by the laws of society, and since marriage among Christians was raised by Christ

[1] *Summa Contra Gentiles*, IV, 78: "Oportet quod . . . a diversis dirigatur. In quantum igitur ordinatur ad bonum naturae, quod est perpetuitas speciei, dirigitur in finem a natura inclinante in hunc finem, et sic dicitur esse naturae officium. In quantum vero ordinatur ad bonum politicum, subiacet ordinationi civilis legis. In quantum ordinatur ad bonum Ecclesiae, oportet quod subiaceat regimini ecclesiastico."

to the dignity of a sacrament of the New Law, the authority by which such marriage is regulated can be none other than that of the Church. For it was to the Church that Christ committed the power of ruling, administering, and teaching in regard to so sacred a contract. As Pope Leo XIII says: "Christ, therefore, having renewed marriage to such and so great excellence, commended and entrusted all the discipline bearing upon these matters to His Church." [2] The same general principle is contained in canon 1016 of the Code of Canon Law: "The marriage of baptized persons is regulated not only by the divine law, but also by canon law, with full recognition accorded however to the competence of the civil power over the merely civil effects of marriage."

The divine law, whether the natural law written in the hearts of men or the positive law as divinely revealed, in and of itself binds all men whether baptized or unbaptized.[3] For the authentic determination of the divine law in regard to marriage, the supreme authority of the Church alone is competent to declare when that law prohibits or invalidates a marriage.[4] This right follows from the fact that the only guardian and interpreter of the divine law is the Church of Christ; [5] and is altogether consonant with the mission which the Church has as man's divinely appointed guide to heaven, for "just as the end at which the Church aims is by far the noblest of ends, so is its authority the most exalted of all authority." [6] Hence in rendering such an authentic declaration of the divine law the Church is but making use of her power of teaching, the *potestas magisterii,* committed to her by Christ, for "the Lord Jesus Christ confided to the Church the deposit of faith, in order that she, with the perpetual assistance of the Holy Spirit, may faithfully preserve and expound the revealed doc-

---

[2] Ep. encycl. *Arcanum Divinae,* 10 feb. 1880, §9—*Fontes,* n. 580; *The Pope and the People,* p. 29.

[3] Cathrein, *Philosophia Moralis* (*Cursus Philosophicus, Pars VI,* ed. decima quinta Friburgi Brisgoviae: Herder & Co., 1929), n. 209.

[4] Cf. canon 1038, §1.

[5] Pius XI, ep. encycl. *Casti Connubii,* 31 dec. 1930—*AAS,* XXII (1930), 552.

[6] Leo XIII, ep. encycl. *Immortale Dei,* 1 nov. 1885, §5—*Fontes,* n. 592; *The Pope and the People,* p. 50.

trine."[7] Concrete examples of the use of this authority may be found in the application of the principles of canons 1060 and 1071, when the Church determines that, unless certain precautions are taken to obviate the danger of perversion, mixed marriages are forbidden by the divine law; likewise, when she declares in canon 1068, §2, that marriage is not to be forbidden if there is a doubt in regard to the impediment of impotence.

The Church, then, has full, independent, and exclusive power over the marriages of all baptized persons. This power, it must be noted, is exclusive in regard to all those things which pertain to the sacrament or which are necessarily connected with it; but such exclusive competence does not extend to those things which are connected only accidentally with the marriage bond and which are separable from it. The Church's right, moreover, is proper to her; it is independent of the consent and good will of the secular authority and is not founded in any way on the civil power.[8] For, as Pope Leo XIII explains: "The Church, always and everywhere, has so used her power with reference to the marriages of Christians that men have clearly seen that it belongs to her as of native right; not being made hers by any human grant, but given divinely to her by the will of her Founder."[9]

It has already been observed that marriage is of divine institution and that in Christian marriage there is a special added sacramental dignity. In considering the competence of the Church over marriage one must of necessity keep in mind these fundamental concepts. For it is upon the fact that Christ raised marriage when entered into by baptized persons from its natural plane to the dignity of a sacrament, and upon the principle that for baptized persons the contract and the sacrament are in-

---

[7] Canon 1322, §1; Chelodi, *Ius Matrimoniale* (ed. quarta, Tridenti: Libreria Moderna Editrice A. Ardesi, 1937), n. 11.

[8] Cf. Pius IX, "*Syllabus Errorum,*" prop. 69—Denzinger-Bannwart-Umberg, *Enchiridion Symbolorum Definitionum et Declarationum de Rebus Fidei et Morum* (21-23. ed., Friburgi Brisgoviae: Herder & Co., 1937), n. 1769. (Hereafter this work will be cited as Denzinger.)

[9] Ep. encycl. *Arcanum Divinae,* 10 feb. 1880, §9—*Fontes,* n. 580; *The Pope and the People,* p. 29.

separable,[10] that the competence of the Church over Christian marriages must be determined.

Further, the power of the Church over Christian marriage extends to all baptized persons. There is no distinction between Catholics and baptized non-Catholics in regard to the existence of this right and its possession on the part of the Church. Her authority includes everything that concerns the bond: the exclusive power to establish prohibitive or diriment impediments,[11] the independent right to determine the form essential to validity,[12] and the native prerogative not only to pass judgment on the validity of a particular marriage,[13] but also to break the bond in certain cases.[14]

There are, however, certain limitations, both of kind and of degree, with which the use of the Church's authority in these matters is accompanied. In the first place the divine law, both natural and positive, circumscribes the limits of the Church's right and power, for " the Church must abstain from establishing those absolute impediments which take away from a person the innate right of marrying which he has from nature "; [15] and the Church must also forego any and every attempt to dissolve the bond of a ratified marriage, once such a valid union has been consummated.[16] In the second place the Church has seen fit to impose upon herself definite restrictions in her exercise of authority over certain classes of marriages which in strict principle, that is, apart from the established restrictions, would be subject to her authority. She has limited the application of her law not only when there is question of the intermarriage of a person of non-Catholic baptism and a person of no baptism at all, as long as

[10] Canon 1012; cf. also Pius IX, "*Syllabus errorum,*" props. 65 and 66—Denzinger, n. 1765 and n. 1766.

[11] Conc. Trident., sess. xxiv, *de matrimonio,* can. 4; *canon* 1038, §2.

[12] Cf. the decrees *Tametsi* and *Ne temere;* canons 1094–1099.

[13] Conc. Trident., sess. xxiv, *de matrimonio,* can. 12; Pius IX, "*Syllabus errorum,*" prop. 74—Denzinger, n. 1774; canon 1960.

[14] For example, in the dissolution of a *matrimonium ratum et non consummatum.* Cf. canon 1119.

[15] Ayrinhac-Lydon, *Marriage Legislation* (new revised ed., New York: Benziger Brothers, 1938), 13.

[16] Canon 1013, §2, and canon 1118; cf. also Matthew, 19:6.

the baptized person has not been converted to the Church,[17] but also when there is question of the intermarriage of persons baptized as non-Catholics, as long as neither of them was ever converted to the Church, and likewise for the case of the intermarriage of persons who in their infancy were baptized in the Church, if as the offspring of non-Catholic or apostate parents they were from childhood reared in a false religion or without any religion at all.[18]

So much, then, for the authority of the Church over the marriages contracted between baptized persons. What of the authority of the State over such marriages? Since the State enjoys competence over only those things that are primarily civil and temporal, it follows that there is lacking to the State any authority over things purely spiritual, such as the sacraments. The State lacks this authority precisely regarding the marriages between Christians, for, as Pope Leo XIII points out: ". . . through the addition of the sacrament the marriages of Christians have become far the noblest of all matrimonial unions. But to decree and ordain concerning the sacrament is, by the will of Christ Himself, so much a part of the power and duty of the Church, that it is plainly absurd to maintain that even the very smallest fraction of such power has been transferred to the civil ruler."[19] The State, therefore, has no power over the bond of sacramental marriages, and cannot establish impediments (either prohibitive or diriment), or legislate in regard to the form, or pass on the validity of such marriages. But since marriage, though a sacrament among the baptized, also concerns civil society, the State is competent over the purely civil or temporal effects of these marriages.[20]

This right of the civil authority has been recognized and is supported by the Church. For the Church, so says Pope Leo

---

17 "Nullum est matrimonium contractum a persona non baptizata cum persona baptizata in Ecclesia catholica vel ad eandem ex haeresi aut schismate conversa."—Canon 1070, §1.

18 Canon 1099, §2.

19 Ep. encycl. *Arcanum Divinae,* 10 feb. 1880, §11—*Fontes,* n. 580; *The Pope and the People,* p. 32.

20 Canon 1016.

XIII, "is not unaware, and never calls in doubt, that the sacrament of marriage, being instituted for the preservation and increase of the human race, has a necessary relation to circumstances of life, which, though connected with marriage, belong to the civil order, and about which the State rightly makes strict inquiry and justly promulgates decrees." [21] It must be remembered that the *purely civil effects* of marriage are definitely circumscribed, and that the right of the State cannot be extended to those effects of Christian marriage which are intrinsically connected with and invariably consequent upon the marital contract.[22] Hence, in relation to Christian marriage the civil authority is incompetent to rule on questions regarding the legitimacy of the offspring, or to grant permission for the parties to separate even temporarily.

Article 2

The Competent Authority over the Marriages between the Unbaptized

It has already been observed that marriage as an institution of the natural law is subject to the laws of God, but that these laws require a more specific determination and application by competent human authority. What, then, is the competent authority over the marriages between unbaptized persons? The unbaptized, no less than Christians, are essentially bound to the same degree by the precepts of the divine law, in particular with regard to the ends and essential properties of marriage; in relation to the diriment impediments of impotence and previous bond, and, in some degrees, of consanguinity; with reference to the necessity of true consent; and with respect to the separation of consorts.[23]

The principle is stated in canon 1038, §1, that the supreme authority of the Church alone has the right to declare authentically

---

[21] Ep. encycl. *Arcanum Divinae,* §21—*Fontes,* n. 580; *The Pope and the People,* p. 40.

[22] Cf. Chapter II, *supra,* p. 25.

[23] Payen, *De Matrimonio in Missionibus et Potissimum in Sinis Tractatus Practicus et Casus* (2. ed., 3 vols., Zi-ka-wei: In typographia T'ou-sè-wè, 1935–1936), I, n. 190.

in which cases the divine law forbids the contracting of marriage or nullifies the attempt of contracting it. That this magisterial authority of the Church extends to the unbaptized as well as to Christians is evident from a comparison of the two paragraphs of canon 1038. For, whereas in the second paragraph the exclusive competence of the Church to establish diriment impediments of ecclesiastical law is restricted to the baptized, in the first paragraph her authority is asserted without any restriction.[24] Hence the unbaptized are subject to the observance of whatever impediments the divine law has established, not only for the cases in which such impediments are manifest and recognized apart from any authoritative declaration, but also for the cases in which the existence of these impediments becomes known through the authentic declaration of the Church in view of her sovereign and exclusive competence in this regard.

As to the binding force of other laws of the Code, the Church has never considered unbaptized persons as direct subjects of her legislation. That general rule is to be found in the prescriptions of canon 12: "Unbaptized persons are not bound by laws that are purely ecclesiastical laws . . ." If the Church, then, recognizes certain limits within her competence over the marriages of the unbaptized, such marriages must either remain under the divine law alone or else be governed also by the civil authority. But the ordinance of reason and the demand of the public good clearly indicate that beyond the need already met by the divine law there still is need for some further positive prescriptions in the right ordering of these marriages. And, indeed, the common opinion among the older canonists and theologians and also among the authors of today is that the State has the right to legislate for the marriages of the unbaptized among themselves, even to the extent of establishing diriment impediments or invalidating laws for such marriages.[25]

---

[24] Vromant, *Ius Missionariorum de Matrimonio* (ed. altera emendata, Parisiis: Desclée, 1938), n. 10.

[25] This opinion is supported by: Sanchez, *De Sancto Matrimonii Sacramento* (Antverpiae, 1652), lib. VII, disp. 3, n. 2; Pirhing, *Ius Canonicum Nova Methodo Explicatum* (5 vols., Dilingae, 1674–1678), lib. IV, tit. 1, section V, n. 151; (It should be noted that Pirhing and Sanchez attribute to

Granted the existence of this competence on the part of the State, it is important for the purpose of the present investigation to determine the nature of this authority or right and, in a general way, the extent to which it may be applied.[26] From what has been said of the nature of marriage it is evident that the marital contract is not merely another civil contract.[27] The natural bond of marriage, even among the unbaptized, is a contract *sui generis;* there is no real parity between it and other contracts. In speaking of marriage as an institution that has God as its author, Pope Leo XIII says that ". . . there abides in it a something holy and religious; not extraneous, but innate; not derived from men, but implanted by nature," and adds further that ". . . marriage is holy by its own power, in its own nature, and of itself." [28]

Hence, since marriage is of its very nature sacred, only some religious authority would *ex iure proprio et nativo* be competent to regulate marriages among the unbaptized. The Church, however, has indicated her own incompetence to rule directly over these marriages. But to say that there exists no authority which

---

the civil authority the same power over the marriages of baptized persons.); Schmalzgrueber, *Ius Ecclesiasticum Universum* (5 vols. in 12, Romae, 1843–1845), lib. IV, tit. 1, n. 367; Wernz, *Ius Matrimoniale,* n. 75; Cappello, *De Sacramentis,* III, nn. 75–76; Vromant, *De Matrimonio,* nn. 13–16; Chelodi, *Ius Matrimoniale,* n. 13; Payen, *De Matrimonio,* I, nn. 204–207; Vlaming, *Praelectiones Iuris Matrimonialis* (3. ed., 2 vols., Bussum in Hollandia, 1919–1921), I, n. 51; Gasparri, *Tractatus Canonicus de Matrimonio* (Editio nova, 2 vols. in 1, Romae: Typis Polyglottis Vaticanis, 1932), nn. 240 ss.; Wernz-Vidal, *Ius Matrimoniale,* nn. 67 ss.; Vermeersch-Creusen, *Epitome Iuris Canonici* (3 vols., Vol. I, 6. ed., 1937; Vols. II-III, 5. ed., 1936; Mechliniae-Romae: H. Dessain), II, n. 298; Cavagnis, *Institutiones Iuris Publici Ecclesiastici,* III, nn. 184–191; Ottaviani, *Institutiones Iuris Publici Ecclesiastici,* II, n. 340, pp. 222–223; and others.

For a presentation of the historical development of this question and for an explanation of the intrinsic and extrinsic proofs in defense of this theory, the above authors may be consulted. It would be beyond the scope of the present study to treat this aspect of the question in detail.

[26] The more specific application of this right will be considered in Chapter V, *infra.*

[27] Cf. Chapter III, *supra.*

[28] Ep. encycl. *Arcanum Divinae,* 10 feb. 1880, §11—*Fontes,* n. 580; *The Pope and the People,* pp. 31 and 32.

is competent to regulate the marriages of infidels would be to imply that God, from Whom is all power and authority, has failed to provide a source of guidance and supervision for these marriages. A supposition of that kind would obviously be contrary to the wisdom and goodness of God, and is indeed at variance with the fact that God has entrusted the welfare and perfection of man in the temporal and in the spiritual order to two respectively competent authorities.[29]

On the other hand, there exists no religious authority established by God other than that of the Church; and for the unbaptized no such authority exists independent of and distinct from the State, for there are but two specifically distinct perfect societies, viz., the Church and the State.[30] In the absence, therefore, of any such religious authority the State, by reason of necessity and by reason of the public good, is competent to regulate the marriages of the unbaptized. Since, however, this right cannot be said to belong to the State *ex iure proprio et nativo,* it must belong to her *ex iure devolutivo et hypothetico.* In other words, the right would belong properly to some special religious authority if such an authority existed; but since there is wanting among the unbaptized any such authority to rule over a thing that is by its very nature sacred, this right devolves by force of circumstance upon the State.[31]

Just as there are limitations in the authority of the Church over Christian marriage, so too there are certain well defined limits beyond which the State may not rightly extend her competence over marriages among the unbaptized. The civil authority is bound to have due regard for the precepts of the natural and

---

[29] Cf. *supra,* Chapter II, p. 19.

[30] "Et quoniam duae solum dantur specie distinctae societates perfectae, Ecclesia et Status, sequitur omnes alias societates quae existunt in mundo necessario referri et subordinari vel Ecclesiae vel Statui prout bonum temporale vel spirituale prosequuntur."—Ottaviani, *Institutiones Iuris Publici Ecclesiastici,* I, n. 26, section V.

[31] Cf. especially Cappello, *De Sacramentis,* III, n. 78; see also Wernz, *Ius Matrimoniale,* n. 75, note 195; Payen, *De Matrimonio,* I, n 205, and note 2; Gasparri, *De Matrimonio,* n. 241; Ottaviani, *Institutiones Iuris Publici Ecclesiastici,* II, n. 340.

divine positive law. For that reason, then, it must recognize the impediments of the divine law, and may never issue decrees or judgments contrary to these impediments; nor may the State abrogate or change these impediments or dispense from them. The civil authority, moreover, has no power whatsoever to break the bond of marriage. This principle is so clearly enunciated by Pope Pius VI in a letter to the Bishop of Eger (Erlau), Hungary, that Pope Pius XI saw fit to repeat the words of his predecessor in his own famous encyclical on Christian marriage: "Hence it is clear that marriage even in the state of nature and certainly long before it was raised to the dignity of a sacrament was divinely instituted in such a way that it should carry with it a perpetual and indissoluble bond which cannot therefore be dissolved by any civil law. Therefore, although the sacramental element may be absent from a marriage, as is the case among unbelievers, still in such a marriage, inasmuch as it is a true marriage, there must remain and indeed there does remain that perpetual bond which by divine right is so bound up with matrimony from its first institution that it is not subject to any civil power . . ." [32] Further, the State must recognize the authentic interpretation of the divine law as rendered by the Church, which alone is competent to make such interpretation.[33] Finally, when the State legislates for the marriages of her unbaptized subjects, these laws must be becoming, reasonable, possible, and useful, so that they are conducive to the common good.[34]

Article 3

The Competent Authority over the Marriages between the Baptized and the Unbaptized

In the two preceding articles there has been set forth the doctrine concerning the competence of the Church over the marriages between Christians, and regarding the authority of the

[32] Pius XI, ep. encycl. *Casti connubii,* 31 dec. 1930—*AAS* XXII (1930), 551; *Selected Papal Encyclicals* 1896 *to* 1931, I, 16.

[33] Canons 1038, §1, and 1322, §1.

[34] Cf. Cappello, *De Sacramentis,* III, n. 77; Vromant, *De Matrimonio,* n. 17.

State over the marriages between infidels. The question now presents itself: Which of these two authorities is competent to regulate a marriage contracted between two persons, one of whom is baptized and the other unbaptized? Does the Church retain its competence for the Christian, and the State its competence for the infidel, in such a way that the combined requisites enacted by the respective authorities must be fulfilled in order that a marriage entered into by the subjects of the two distinct jurisdictions be a valid marriage? Or may it be said that the competence of one authority must yield place to that of the other, so that one authority alone shall be competent to regulate the marriage?

It is certain that the marriage between a Christian and an infidel is subject to the divine law, and to that extent at least is subject solely to the supreme authority of the Church, which alone has the right to declare the circumstances under which the divine law would render such a marriage illicit or invalid.[35]

It has already been observed that inasmuch as the unbaptized are not subject to her jurisdiction they are not bound *directly* by the marriage laws of the Church. There are, however, certain cases in which the infidel is bound *indirectly* by the legislation of the Church.

Thus, in the first place, if an unbaptized person free of every impediment wishes to contract marriage with a baptized person who under canon law is bound by some impediment, the unbaptized party through the law of the Church indirectly becomes incapacitated for entering into this marriage. This result obtains whether the baptized party is impeded by reason of an impediment entirely proper to himself, as, e.g., the impediment of nonage or of vow (i.e., an *absolute* impediment), or by reason of some impediment which binds him only in relation to the unbaptized party, as, e.g., the impediment of consanguinity or of disparity of worship (i.e., a *relative* impediment). The reason given for this is that the matrimonial contract, being a bilateral agreement, has an absolute indivisibility, so that what affects *directly* one party

[35] Canon 1038, §1.

to the contract affects *indirectly* the other party also.[36] Moreover, the principle is stated in canon 1036, §3, that even when the impediment exists on only one side it renders marriage illicit or invalid for both parties.

Secondly, if an unbaptized person marries a Catholic, he is indirectly subject to the jurisdiction of the Church by the fact that the Catholic form of marriage must be observed.[37] One may readily allow for further instances of the undisputed competence of the Church over the marriage between a Christian and an infidel in matrimonial causes and in the exercise of the ministerial power of the Church.[38]

The Church, as has already been seen, is exclusively competent to establish matrimonial impediments for Christians. The State, therefore, may not establish any *relative* impediment, which, though directly intended for her unbaptized subjects, would, nevertheless, bind indirectly the baptized party to a marriage. This limitation upon the right of the State flows not only from the fact that her power to establish impediments is restricted to the marriages of infidels *among themselves,* but also from the fact that her right to regulate such marriages belongs to the State not *ex iure proprio et nativo* but only *ex iure devolutivo et hypothetico.*[39] Furthermore, any attempt on the part of the civil authority to establish such a relative impediment would be an infringement upon the jurisdiction over Christian marriage which Christ committed exclusively to His Church.

But, on the other hand, the problem arising from *absolute* impediments established by the State for her unbaptized subjects is not so readily solved. It is sharply controverted whether an absolute diriment impediment decreed by the State and binding only the unbaptized party in a mixed marriage, would render invalid such a union, notwithstanding the fact that the baptized

---

[36] Cf. Wernz, *Ius Matrimoniale,* n. 40, Scholion; Cappello, *De Sacramentis,* III, n. 67, 5°; Payen, *De Matrimonio,* I, n. 200, 2°; Gasparri, *De Matrimonio,* n. 256.

[37] Canon 1099, §1, 2°.

[38] Cf. Payen, *De Matrimonio,* I, n. 200, note 1, 3°; Cappello, *De Sacramentis,* III, n. 67, 3° and 4°.

[39] Cf. *supra,* pp. 43 and 45.

party was free of, or dispensed from, canonical impediments. At the present the question remains an open issue, for the Holy See has not as yet made any official declaration that has definitely settled the controversy.

Among those canonists who defend the opinion that an absolute civil diriment impediment which binds only the unbaptized party would invalidate his attempted marriage with a baptized party, may be cited Gasparri,[40] Vlaming,[41] De Becker,[42] Vermeersch-Creusen,[43] Onclin [44] and Oesterle.[45]

The opposite opinion holds that the Church alone is competent to establish diriment impediments which would invalidate a marriage between a baptized party and an unbaptized party, and that consequently any civil law affecting the validity of such a marriage through the unbaptized party would cease to bind. This view is supported by Wernz,[46] Wernz-Vidal,[47] Payen,[48] Chelodi,[49] Cappello,[50] Vromant,[51] Alford,[52] Grandclaude,[53] and De Smet.[54]

The proponents of the first opinion—that the civil impediment

[40] *De Matrimonio,* n. 256.

[41] *Praelectiones Iuris Matrimonii,* n. 195.

[42] *De Matrimonio Praelectiones Canonicae* (Editio nova, Louvain: Fr. Ceuterick, 1931), 25–26.

[43] *Epitome,* II, n. 278.

[44] "De Regimine Matrimonii Fidelem inter et Infidelem"—*Ephemerides Theologicae Lovanienses* (Lovanii: Universitas Catholica Lovanienses, 1924–), X (1933), 47–62.

[45] "De iure in missionibus matrimoniali"—*Commentarium pro Religiosis et Missionariis* (Romae, 1920–), XVII (1936), 257–270.

[46] *Ius Matrimoniale,* n. 60.

[47] *Ius Matrimoniale,* n. 52.

[48] *De Matrimonio,* I, n. 202.

[49] *Ius Matrimoniale,* n. 12.

[50] *De Sacramentis,* III, n. 67.

[51] *De Matrimonio,* nn. 5–7.

[52] *Ius Matrimoniale Comparatum* (Romae: Anonima Libraria Cattolica Italiana, 1938), n. 21.

[53] "Compétence de l'État Touchant le Mariage des Infideles"—*Le Canoniste Contemporain,* X (1887), pp. 241–257; Grandclaude, *Ius Canonicum* (3 vols. Parisiis, 1882–1883), III, 33.

[54] *Tractatus Theologico-Canonicus De Sponsalibus et Matrimonio* (ed. quarta inde a Codice altera, Brugis: Car. Beyaert, Editor Pontificius, 1927), n. 412, note 3, and n. 438 *bis.*

is efficacious to invalidate these marriages—base their arguments on the indivisibility of the marriage contract and on the competence of the State to make laws for its unbaptized subjects. It is their view that marriage cannot be validly contracted as long as one of the parties is bound by a diriment impediment; and that, granted the right of the State to establish absolute matrimonial impediments for the unbaptized, it is altogether consonant with reason that the capacity of parties to a marriage between a Christian and an infidel be determined by the proper law—ecclesiastical for the Christian, civil law for the infidel. "For," says Gasparri,[55] "if you admit . . . that the civil authority can establish diriment matrimonial impediments for its own unbaptized subjects, it follows that the marriage in this case would be invalid from canon 1036, §3, unless the civil authority had granted to its unbaptized subject a dispensation, which the Church cannot grant."

Moreover, according to those who favor this opinion, there is no real conflict of jurisdiction involved in such cases; rather, there exists a simultaneous and equally efficacious competence on the part of the Church and on the part of the State. For, so they maintain, impediments are disqualifications of the very persons contracting, and directly regard not the contract itself, but the persons. And hence, even when it is assumed that the contract enjoys a unity and an indivisibility which make it repugnant to reason to admit the possible subjection of the contract to a twofold competence at one and the same time, nevertheless there are in question two distinct persons for each of whom the acknowledged qualification to enter upon a matrimonial contract constitutes a prerequisite condition for the lawful or valid making of that contract. But the determining of the qualifications of the two contracting parties is not a matter which cannot be divided between two competencies. Hence this matter can be regulated separately as it affects the two separate individuals subject to the two separate authorities.[56]

---

[55] *Loc. cit.*

[56] Cf. especially Onclin, "De Regimine Matrimonii Fidelem inter et Infidelem"—*Ephemerides Theologicae Lovanienses,* X (1933), 55–56.

It must certainly be admitted that the arguments offered in support of the first opinion are ably presented. It must also be granted that the arguments themselves are not devoid of all force of conviction. Yet the second view, which holds that in a marriage between a baptized person and an unbaptized person the jurisdiction and competence of the Church must prevail, appears to be the more probable opinion. Its advocates generally propose a threefold argument drawn from the following three considerations: the possible conflict of jurisdiction; the Catholic doctrine on marriage; and the practice of the Church with respect to such marriages.

In the first place, when the same marriage contract, considered under the same aspect, i.e., as efficacious to establish a marital bond, is regulated by two authorities neither of which is directly subject to the other, it cannot but happen that there will sometimes be a conflict of rights and of jurisdiction. But it is not possible that the same marriage should be at the same time subject to the regulations of two independent and distinct authorities; consequently, when such an occasion arises the law of the State ought to yield to the higher law of the Church.[57] This is in accordance with a fundamental juridical principle. "For in any conflict between societies which are formally distinct, the superior one, or that one which has its end in a higher order, should prevail, and to that same society belongs the right to judge the extent and solution of the conflict." [58]

It would, moreover, seem to be a *petitio principii* to maintain with the opponents of this view that there is no real conflict here because the impediments are qualifications of the persons contracting and these qualifications may be determined by the competent authorities of the respective parties. For, after all, these impediments are qualifications not considered abstractly with reference to the juridical status of the persons within their own juridical order, but rather qualifications considered precisely in reference to a particular marriage contracted or to be contracted with a person who is the subject of an independent and distinct

---

57 Cf. especially Payen and De Smet, *loc. cit.*

58 Ottaviani, *Institutiones Iuris Publici Ecclesiastici,* I, n. 82.

juridical society. Moreover, the question at issue is one not of competence over the persons who are parties to the contract, but of competence over the marriage itself; and hence there can be present a real conflict of jurisdiction.

The second argument, based on the doctrine of the sacred character of marriage, is developed in the following manner. The civil authority may not exercise its jurisdiction either directly or, by virtue of the indivisibility of a bilateral contract, indirectly over *sacred matters* of the baptized; nor may its competence extend even indirectly over a *baptized person* in his relation to a contract which is sacred of its very nature. The Church alone has competence over the marriage of a Christian with an infidel both by reason of the matter which is sacred and also by reason of the person who through baptism is a subject of the Church.

With regard to the first of these points, it is observed that such a marriage, although not existing in the Christian as a true sacrament, is for him nonetheless a thing which is "sacred by its own power, in its own nature, and of itself." [59] But the sacred things of Christians are subject to the exclusive jurisdiction of the Church—and this is true also of the sacred matrimonial contract of a baptized person when he marries an unbaptized person.[60] Moreover, it has already been noted that the competence of the State over marriage for the unbaptized among themselves arises from a merely devolved right, or from the absence of a competent authority. But in the case of a marriage between a baptized person and an unbaptized person, "there is present a competent authority, namely the Church, both by reason of the matter and by reason of the indivisibility of the contract, by reason of the necessary connection, and by reason of the necessary forum; hence the competence of the State ceases . . . With the cessation of the State's competence, the impediments and other things required by civil law cease; hence . . . such marriages are regulated exclusively by the norms of canon law." [61]

The second point of this argument is that the Church enjoys

[59] Leo XIII, ep. encycl. *Arcanum Divinae,* 10 feb. 1880, §11—*Fontes,* n. 580.

[60] Cf. Payen and Wernz-Vidal, *loc. cit.*

[61] Alford, *Ius Matrimoniale Comparatum,* n. 21.

proper, ordinary, and exclusive jurisdiction over the baptized party in such a marriage and, consequently, the State cannot extend its authority in any manner so as to include that person. It has already been pointed out that the State cannot establish *relative* matrimonial impediments for the reason that to bind a baptized person even indirectly by matrimonial impediments is beyond its competence. The same argument is valid when an *absolute* impediment is considered in relation to a particular marriage between a Christian and an infidel. Although in the abstract an absolute impediment affects only one party, yet in the concrete, when a specific marriage is under consideration, the absolute incapacity of one party to marry becomes so specified that indirectly it affects the other party also.[62]

Hence authors conclude that both by reason of the sacred matter and by reason of the baptized person the regulation of the marriage of a baptized party with an unbaptized party is exclusively subject to the authority of the Church just as is the marriage of two Christians.

The third argument of those who favor the exclusive competence of the Church over such marriages is drawn as a confirmatory argument from the practice of the Church in granting dispensations and in asserting her sole judicial authority over marriages between a Christian and an infidel. The fact that the Church repeatedly grants to Catholics dispensations from the impediment of disparity of worship without making inquiry as to whether or not the unbaptized party is bound by any absolute civil diriment impediment indicates that she does not regard such an impediment as capable of having any effect on the validity of such a mixed marriage. For, certainly if these impediments were considered as efficacious to invalidate a marriage under these circumstances, the Church would exercise every care to investigate the status of the infidel with respect to the civil impediments to which he would be subject in consequence of that consideration.

---

[62] Dillon, *Common Law Marriage* (The Catholic University of America Canon Law Studies, n. 153, Washington, D. C.: The Catholic University of America Press, 1942), 81; cf. also Vromant, *De Matrimonio,* nn. 5–7.

Furthermore, since the Church asserts her exclusive judicial competence over marriages between the baptized and the unbaptized on the grounds that she alone is competent to judge all matrimonial causes of the baptized, it is concluded that she also enjoys exclusive legislative competence over these same marriages, because "exclusive judicial power supposes exclusive legislative power: for the right of the forum follows from the right to make laws." [63]

In support of the opinion favoring the Church as the competent authority over marriage between the baptized and the unbaptized, three documents are generally cited by the authors: (1°) The Constitution *Singulari nobis* of Pope Benedict XIV in which, writing about a mixed marriage between a Christian woman and a Jew, he denied the competence of the civil authority over such a marriage.[64] (2°) A response of the Sacred Congregation of the Holy Office on September 20, 1854, which in speaking of a marriage of two infidels, invalidly contracted because of a civil impediment, declared that if either party were converted, the consent was to be renewed after a dispensation was obtained from *ecclesiastical* impediments. No reference was made to the diriment impediment established by the civil law.[65] (3°) A reply of the Sacred Congregation for the Propagation of the Faith on April 1, 1816, which declared that marriages contracted *in facie Ecclesiae* cannot be invalidated by civil law.[66]

From the arguments adduced and from the confirmatory practice and documents of the Church, it appears very tenable that the common and more probable opinion is the one which holds that when one of the contracting parties is baptized and the other unbaptized, the marriage, whether already contracted or to be contracted, is under the exclusive competence of the Church, just as is a marriage between two Christians, and the civil authority is competent only in regard to the purely civil effects.

---

[63] Wernz-Vidal, *Ius Matrimoniale,* n. 52; cf. also Payen, *De Matrimonio,* I, n. 202.

[64] 9 feb. 1749, §7—*Fontes,* n. 394.

[65] *Collectanea,* I, n. 1104; *Fontes,* n. 928; and cf. Vromant, *loc. cit.*

[66] *Collectanea,* I, n. 711; *Fontes,* n. 4703; and cf. Vromant, *loc. cit.*

CHAPTER V

PARTICULAR PROBLEMS AND DISPUTED POINTS OF COMPETENCE

In setting forth the fundamental juridical principles that govern the relations of Church and State as perfect and necessary juridical societies, the writer has pointed out that each is supreme in its own order. By the designs of God's Providence each has its own sphere and province of authority within which the spiritual and temporal welfare of the human race is respectively and adequately cared for. "But," as Pope Leo XIII observes, "inasmuch as each of these two powers has authority over the same subjects, and as it might come to pass that one and the same thing—related differently, but still remaining one and the same thing—might belong to the jurisdiction and determination of both, therefore God, who foresees all things, and who is the Author of these two powers, has marked out the course of each in right correlation to the other." [1]

The orderly connection that should exist between these two authorities can be maintained only if they work together harmoniously and in a spirit of co-operation towards the attainment of their respective aims and purposes. This spirit of reciprocal assistance and mutual respect can be, and often is, further strengthened in regard to particular matters by the establishing of concordats between the rulers of the State and the Roman Pontiff.[2]

Matrimony has been shown to be a matter which, under different aspects, comes under the competence of both Church and State. In regard to a matter which, albeit in different ways, is of common right and authority, it is extremely important that union and concord be maintained between these two perfect societies. For,

[1] Ep. encycl. *Immortale Dei,* 1 nov. 1885, §6—*Fontes,* n. 592; *The Pope and the People,* pp. 51-52.

[2] Cf. Leo XIII, ep. encycl. *Immortale Dei,* §6—*Fontes,* n. 592.

again, as Leo XIII so poignantly remarks: " In matters of mixed jurisdiction, it is in the highest degree consonant to nature, as also to the designs of God, that so far from one of the powers separating itself from the other, or still less coming into conflict with it, complete harmony, such as is suited to the end for which each power exists, should be preserved between them." [3] Such are, indeed, the ideal conditions and the principles under which Church and State should function, especially in their relations with each other.

To say that such conditions have not been fostered and that these principles have not been adhered to by the civil authority is obviously a truism. Far from any such adherence there has rather been developed and encouraged the concept of a purely secularized State, in which authority is considered as derived from the will of the people, and in which the Church is regarded merely as another of the inferior societies within the State and therefore as having no right or power except what she holds by the concession and favor of the civil government. The consequent lack of respect for the rights and prerogatives of the Church, and the absence of a proper sense of her own responsibilities on the part of the State, have produced lamentable results. And in no aspect of their mutual relations and obligations has more harm been done by these erroneous theories than in matters of twofold jurisdiction—especially in regard to the sacred matrimonial contract. " With reference to matters that are of twofold jurisdiction, they who administer the civil power lay down the law at their own will, and in matters that appertain to religion defiantly put aside the most sacred decrees of the Church. They claim jurisdiction over the marriages of Catholics, even over the bond as well as the unity and indissolubility of matrimony." [4]

---

[3] Ep. encycl. *Immortale Dei,* §17—*Fontes,* n. 592; *The Pope and the People,* p. 62.

[4] Leo XIII, ep. encycl. *Immortale Dei,* §11—*Fontes,* n. 592; *The Pope and the People,* p. 58. Cf. also the same Pontiff's ep. encycl. *Arcanum Divinae—Fontes,* n. 580, *passim,* and Pius XI, ep. encycl. *Casti Connubii—AAS,* XXII (1930), pp. 539-592, *passim*—both treating of Christian Marriage; also Pius XI, ep. encycl. *Divini illius Magistri,* 31 dec. 1929—*AAS,* XXII (1930), pp. 49-86, *passim*—on the Christian Education of Youth.

Out of these undesirable conditions have arisen many practical problems of competence. In our own country the civil authorities in legislating for marriage have not hesitated to apply their laws to all subjects of the State, irrespective of the rights of the Church over the baptized. These laws touch upon prerequisites for marriage, upon the form of marriage, upon matrimonial impediments, and even upon the dissolution of the marital contract. To many of these laws, moreover, there are attached penalties to be imposed on those who fail to observe them. For both priests and laity the practical difficulty of adhering to principles which may not be compromised, and yet of avoiding open defiance of civil requirements and prohibitions, immediately presents itself. Catholics wish to live peaceably in accordance with the just law of the land, and in a spirit of charity will even submit to civil regulations which, though invalid for them (because to legislate for them in these particular matters is outside the competence of the civil authority), may yet be accepted as just and proper in that they are not contrary to the natural law and the divine positive law. Indeed, the Church generally permits this observance for the purpose of avoiding greater evil. But certainly those laws which are directly opposed to the natural or divine positive law are binding on no one; and those laws which are direct contraventions of purely ecclesiastical laws are surely not binding on subjects of the Church.[5]

It remains now to consider in detail the practical problems and disputed points of competence. This will be undertaken by means of viewing the various requirements of civil law in the United States in the light of the principles already established.

Article 1

Civil Prerequisites for Marriage

In every State and Territory of the United States there exist laws which require that those who wish to contract marriage obtain from the competent civil official a document showing that the civil authority has been notified of the intended marriage, and

[5] Cf. Cavagnis, *Institutiones Iuris Publici Ecclesiastici,* III, n. 197; Ottaviani, *Institutiones Iuris Publici Ecclesiastici,* II, n. 340, p. 222.

attesting that so far as civil laws are concerned there appears to be no obstacle to the marriage, and stating that it is lawful for a competent minister to assist at the wedding. In most of these states this document is designated as a *marriage license;* but in some it is termed simply a *certificate.* In some of the states the license is required only for the lawfulness, but in others for the validity of the marriage.[6]

Insofar as the document itself is concerned, if it is to be called a "license," then the term must be understood in a broad sense. The right that man has to marry comes to him from the natural law and not through the concession of any human authority. If, moreover, the license be regarded as a declaration that the parties are free of any civil impediments and may therefore contract marriage, it can be understood as applying in that sense only to the unbaptized, who alone are subject to such civil impediments. *De facto,* however, the license does not prove that there is no impediment to the marriage. It merely shows that, so far as the civil laws are concerned, it appears to the civil authority that these parties are capable of contracting marriage legitimately.[7]

Only the Church can establish, within the limits already noted, impediments for Christian marriages,[8] and consequently the baptized are not bound by these civil impediments. For the baptized, then, the license itself can at most be regarded only as the first step in the civil registration of the marriage. It is fully within the competence of the State to require registration of all marriages, even those of the baptized, in order that the purely civil effects that follow from the marital contract may receive legal sanction and recognition. This registration of the marriage is usually completed through the filing with the proper civil official of a formal certification or notification which is signed by the assisting minister and which testifies that the marriage has actually been contracted. And it is further within the power of the civil authority to decree and inflict penalities upon the parties for non-observance of these solemnities required by the civil law.

---

[6] Alford, *Ius Matrimoniale Comparatum,* nn. 284 and 287.

[7] Cf. Alford, *op. cit.,* n. 284.

[8] Cf. Chapter IV, *supra,* pp. 38–41.

But these penalties may never extend to the point of declaring that the marriage will be illicit or invalid in civil law unless such registration has been made.[9] Nor has the State any *right* to punish a priest for his failure to observe these prescriptions of the civil law; to do so would be to interfere with the exercise of his ecclesiastical ministry and would militate against the freedom and independence of the Church.[10] In this country, however, where in many of the states there actually do exist penal sanctions in these matters directed against the minister as well as against the parties, prudence would dictate that priests regard compliance with such regulations as a conscientious duty—if not to protect themselves, at least to prevent serious harm to the parties and to their children.[11]

Furthermore, in denying legal recognition of the effects of marriage to those parties who have not complied with the civil laws on registration, the State exceeds its authority when it refuses to recognize the legitimacy of the children born of a marriage between two Christians and (according to the common and more probable opinion[12]) of a marriage between a baptized person and an unbaptized person. For the legitimacy of children is not one of the merely civil effects of marriage, but rather is one of the effects that is inseparable from the substance of the contract, and consequently in such cases lies within the province of the authority of the Church. But in the event of conflict by reason of State legislation on this matter, the parties should attempt, insofar as this be possible, to see to it that the legitimacy of the children be established in the civil forum also; this obligation arises not from the force of the civil laws themselves, but rather

---

[9] "Quae poenae nunquam eo extendi possunt, ut matrimonium nonnisi a tempore registrationis civilis in foro saeculari habeatur valide et licite celebratum."—Wernz, *Ius Matrimoniale,* n. 83.

[10] Cavagnis, *Institutiones Iuris Publici Ecclesiastici,* III, n. 207.

[11] Cf. Nau, *Marriage Laws of the Code* (2. ed., New York and Cincinnati: Pustet, 1934), n. 11; Alford, *Ius Matrimoniale Comparatum,* n. 12.

[12] Cf. Chapter IV, *supra,* p. 49, for authors who hold this opinion and for those who hold the opposite view.

from a duty in charity to avoid consequent grave harm to their children.[13]

Before the issuance of the marriage license or certificate itself, certain antecedent requirements are prescribed by the law of some states. One such prerequisite is the *declaration of intention* that is to be made by the parties. In a very general way this requirement may be said to correspond to the *publication of the banns* in Church law. The object of this declaration of intention is to restrain the contracting parties from hasty and inadvisable marriages and to provide some time for investigation as to the capacity of the parties to marry. To that end the regulation demands that there be a certain interval of time between the declaration of intention and the obtaining of a license, or between the obtaining of a license and the actual contracting of marriage.[14]

This interval of time varies in the respective states. Some permit the issuing of a license immediately upon the notification of intention to marry, and also the subsequent marriage without further delay; among the other states, the interval of time ranges in length from one to thirty days.[15] Among those states which require longer intervals, there is usually some provision for exceptions to be made under certain circumstances, as, e.g., when there exists a good or reasonable cause for immediate marriage. These causes are frequently specified in the laws of the several states. These various regulations governing the declaration of intention of the parties are in themselves just and reasonable, and hence unbaptized subjects of the State who wish to contract marriage are bound to observe them. It is another matter for the baptized subjects of the State, because these particular marriage

---

[13] Cf. Benedictus XIV, ep., *Redditae sunt,* 17 sept. 1746, §3—*Fontes,* n. 372; S.C.S. Off. (Vic. Ap. Jamaicae), 12 ian. 1881—*Fontes,* n. 1069; Cappello, *De Sacramentis,* III, n. 74, 3º; Payen, *De Matrimonio,* I, n. 199, note 5; Alford, *Ius Matrimoniale Comparatum,* n. 264.

[14] Cf. Alford, *Ius Matrimoniale Comparatum,* sectio 27, *passim.*

[15] This is but one of many concrete examples of the need for uniform marriage legislation among the states. The law of one state may be evaded by the parties' going into another state where no such interval is demanded, and there obtaining a license and being married immediately. In such a way the whole purpose of the law may be easily defeated.

laws have no binding force in themselves for citizens who are at the same time subjects of the Church, *except and only* insofar as they are concerned with the purely civil effects of marriage. To that extent and to the extent that these regulations are just and valid (i.e., do not interfere with the higher rights of the Church), they are in themselves also binding upon the baptized subjects of the State.

When, however, the scope of this legislation extends beyond the merely civil effects and touches upon either the substance itself or upon the inseparable effects of the marital bond, the obligation arising from the civil law to observe these regulations is no longer binding upon Christians. But in such an eventuality—since the connection between these antecedent requirements and the issuance of the license itself is so close—the same principle that was employed above may be applied here. Consequently, for the purpose of avoiding serious harm to themselves or to their children, the Christian parties (or, in the case of a mixed marriage, the Christian and the infidel) may be said to be bound by a precept of charity to comply with these regulations; but, obviously, their failure to do so would have no effect on the validity or the lawfulness of their marriage. For it must be borne in mind, as Pope Leo XIII has indicated, that, although the civil power can set up and regulate the civil effects of marriage, nevertheless what proximately concerns marriage itself must be left to the jurisdiction of the Church.[16]

Another necessary condition for the obtaining of a license is the *approbation of the parents* which is required of the parties intending to be married if they have not attained the legal age for marriage according to the civil statutes.[17] This prescription is not concerned with the impediment of nonage; it is directed rather towards the period between the cessation of that impediment and the attaining of the age that establishes a person in his

[16] Leo XIII, litt. *Il divisamento,* 8 feb. 1893, n. 2: ". . . ma non è inopportuno dichiarare anche una volta, che il potere civile disponga pure dei civili effetti del matrimonio, ma lasci alla chiesa ciò che riguarda il matrimonio in se stesso."—*Fontes,* n. 617.

[17] Generally, this legal age is twenty-one years for men and eighteen years for women. Cf. Alford, *Ius Matrimoniale Comparatum,* n. 301.

legal majority. It is simply a restriction on the freedom of minors to marry, and it decrees that the ones thus restricted must obtain the consent of their parents or guardian before they will be granted a license to marry. There is little practical conflict between the civil and the canonical legislation on this point, for the requirements of the various states in this regard usually affect only the question of lawfulness for the marriage which is contracted in contravention of them. In the event, however, that this civil regulation should be extended to touch upon the bond itself, it would not affect the validity of a Christian marriage contracted in accordance with the laws of the Church, even though the parental consent had not been obtained. For, in canon law, the consent of parents is required only for the lawfulness of the marriage—and, indeed, not always for the lawfulness because lack of parental consent is not a prohibitive impediment properly so called.[18]

Of the various civil prerequisites for marriage perhaps the most important is the one derived from the so-called *eugenic legislation,* by which persons suffering from venereal infection are forbidden to marry as long as they have the disease. This regulation may well be, and often is, treated along with other civil impediments under the caption "impediment of disease." In the present study, however, it will be examined at this point as one of the prerequisites for marriage, since the usual procedure of this eugenic legislation is to require that those who intend to be married secure from a physician a written statement certifying that they are free from venereal diseases. This certificate must be presented to the proper civil official before the parties can obtain a marriage license.

---

[18] Canon 1034.

The question may arise as to whether a priest should marry a person who has obtained a license by lying about his having reached his legal majority. Because of the manifold possible variations and circumstances among concrete cases, it would be quite difficult to make an answer sufficiently comprehensive to include all such cases. Bearing in mind the fundamental principles of competence, the priest, when confronted with a problem of this kind, will have to determine his course of action by applying the regulations of canon law and the principles of moral theology to the specific case.

These laws are variously designated as "eugenic laws" or "social disease laws" or "blood-test laws." Like most of the other civil laws on marriage in this country, they vary widely among the different states. Here, as before, the present purpose is not to examine in detail the diverse specific requirements; it is rather to consider the broader aspects of the nature and aim of the legislation, and to determine the rights and competence of Church and State in the light of fundamental juridical principles. Indeed, the particular importance of the eugenic laws for this study arises from the practical conflict of jurisdiction that they present—a conflict that comes about more by virtue of the form of the legislation and the manner of its application than by reason of the sociological aims and purposes that underlie it.

Hence, although it would be out of place to discuss here the biological and sociological factors that may be involved, it must be remarked that the ravages of social disease in this country are such as to manifest the real need for concerted effort on the part of civil authorities to eliminate by every lawful means this great scourge. But the emphasis from the juridic standpoint is to be placed on the fact that this must be accomplished by *lawful means;* the need for legislation in the matter, however great it may be, does not in any wise warrant an infringement by the State on the authority and jurisdiction of the Church.

Eugenic laws, like other marriage laws in this country, have been legislated by the states without due regard for the rights of the Church. They have been made binding on all subjects of the State, baptized and unbaptized alike. It is clear from the principles already set forth that the Church alone is competent to establish impediments, diriment or impedient, for Christian marriages. Hence the civil authority may not prescribe a medical examination for baptized persons about to be married in such wise that, if this condition is not fulfilled, marriage is forbidden to them. By so doing the State would be establishing an impediment, and this the State is entirely incompetent to do for such marriages.[19] For an attempt to legislate in such a manner

19 "Quoad baptizatos, nequit tale examen praescribere ita, ut *non servata hac conditione,* matrimonium ipsis esset interdictum . . . sic enim directe vel

constitutes a transgression of the order of authority as established by God. It is recognized, however, that the civil power does enjoy competence over the merely civil effects of marriage.

By virtue of that authority may not the State, then, for reasons of the common good, and particularly for the purpose of promoting and insuring the health of its citizens, enact such restrictions? Certainly it must be said that "if the civil authorities concerned themselves with the *merely* natural aspects of the matter—for example, by instructing the citizens about the nature and the virulence of social diseases and by providing remedies for them—the state would be acting within its proper sphere." [20] But to go beyond this in any way so as to touch upon the supernatural marital bond would be to exceed the limits of its authority with respect to the civil effects. Hence, to decree that, if the medical certificate is not obtained, the marriage either will not be civilly recognized or will be deprived of some of its essential and intrinsic effects, or even to impose upon the baptized this medical examination under penalty of denial of the merely civil effects, would be equivalent to the establishment, at least indirectly, of an impediment. This, again, it is not within the competence of the State to do.[21]

It is admitted that the State would act entirely within its proper sphere of authority if it segregated diseased persons until such time that they can be cured of the venereal infection. Yet it does not follow from that that it also lies within the power of the State to restrain them from marrying without such segregation. It is one thing for persons to be rendered incapable of marrying as a *consequence* of the lawful exercise of proper civil authority, for then the act of marrying on the part of such persons would become illicit only accidentally and by reason of some extrinsic circumstance, but not essentially so or in view of the act itself

saltem indirecte impedimentum dirimens vel prohibens constitueret, ad quod prorsus incompetens est."—Aertnys-Damen, *Theologia Moralis* (12. ed., 2 vols., Taurinorum Augustae: Marietti, 1932), II, n. 636.

[20] Connell, "May the State Forbid Marriage because of Social Disease?"—*The Ecclesiastical Review* (Philadelphia, 1889—), XCIX (1938), 512.

[21] Cf. Aertnys-Damen, *Theologia Moralis,* II, n. 636.

independently of other factors. But it is quite another matter for such persons to be prohibited from marrying by direct legislative action which touches upon the marriage contract itself, for it is wrong to deduce from the above accidental and extrinsic right that the State can make regulations for a supernatural and sacramental thing, when its power extends to that sacred thing not insofar as it is sacred but only by reason of extrinsic circumstances.[22]

The principles thus far applied to the social disease laws, as legislated in this country, present no particular difficulty or ground for dispute in regard to their application. But at least one author, on the ground of the State's power to enforce the natural law, seems ready to vindicate its right to make such health laws. It is maintained that the State may use its legislative and coercive powers with regard to what is prescribed or forbidden by the natural law concerning marriage insofar as violations of that law are harmful to the good of society.[23] Donnelly (who supports this opinion) holds that in view of the highly infectious character of social disease an infected person may not marry one who is free of the disease, for the subsequent cohabitation and relationship of such parties would be unsafe for the healthy partner. Such a danger, he says, must be avoided on the grounds that the natural right to marry may not be exercised in a way that would cause injury to others. Hence, " the State may use

---

[22] " Aliae sunt dispositiones quae requiruntur pro ordinata et honesta susceptione alicuius sacramenti, et in genere pro cuiuscumque negotii expeditione, attenta tantum rei natura, et aliae quae per accidens supervenire possunt ex extrinsecis adiunctis; iudicium de illis vel ordinatio positiva in re religiosa ad Ecclesiam spectat; quoad secundas locum habere potest et iustum praeceptum alterius auctoritatis, puta patrisfamilias, aut principis de cuius tamen iustitia iudicare semper spectat ad Ecclesiam, tamquam ad supremum moralitatis tribunal."—Cavagnis, *Institutiones Iuris Publici Ecclesiastici*, III, n. 196; cf. also Connell, " May the State Forbid Marriage because of Social Disease? "—*The Ecclesiastical Review*, XCIX (1938), 510 and 512.

[23] The pros and cons of this view are ably presented in a recent controversial article on the question. Cf. Donnelly and Connell, " Compulsory Blood Tests before Marriage."—*The Ecclesiastical Review*, CI (1939), 9-30.

its authority even over baptized persons to prevent injury from being inflicted."[24]

This opinion presupposes that it is against the natural law for a person suffering from a venereal infection to marry. But, while such a moral principle is not entirely lacking in support, the majority of theologians teach that, given the requisite justifying causes, the natural law does not forbid the marriage of a person afflicted with a communicable social disease.[25] Granted the power of the State to enforce the natural law for the good of civil society, it is nevertheless necessary to distinguish between the exercise of that power over the baptized and its exercise over the unbaptized. For the baptized, it may be admitted, with Gasparri, the civil authority can under certain circumstances and for the public good enforce a natural law by virtue of which one is obliged to postpone marriage for a time,[26] so long as this power is restricted, as Connell suggests, "to matters prescribed or forbidden by the natural law according to the teachings of the Catholic Church."[27] Donnelly concurs in this aspect of the question, for he says that the State "may not go beyond the limits of natural law as defined by the Church in her official pronouncements and in the approved teaching of her theologians."[28]

But, it must be pointed out, the Church has nowhere declared that the natural law forbids the marriage of persons afflicted with

---

[24] "Compulsory Blood Tests before Marriage."—*The Ecclesiastical Review,* CI (1939), 20.

[25] Cf., e.g., Sabetti-Barrett, *Compendium Theologiae Moralis* (8. ed. post Codicem, Neo Eboraci: Pustet, 1939), n. 842, 6º; Wernz-Vidal, *Ius Matrimoniale,* n. 489.

[26] "At quamquam Princeps nequeat, radicali impossibilitate, pro suis subditis baptizatis impedimenta statuere, quae attingant validitatem aut etiam liceitatem vinculi per se inspectam, tamen potest, in nonnullis circumstantiis, ratione boni publici, urgendo naturae ius, matrimonium ad tempus prohibere vel aliquas determinare conditiones ab illis implendas, qui volunt matrimonium inire; . . ."—*De Matrimonio,* n. 236.

[27] "Compulsory Blood Tests before Marriage."—*The Ecclesiastical Review,* CI (1939), 29.

[28] "Compulsory Blood Tests before Marriage."—*The Ecclesiastical Review,* CI (1939), 20.

social diseases. On the contrary, as Connell declares in another article, "for centuries Catholic theologians have been teaching that marriage and the use of marriage are not prohibited by the divine law when one party is afflicted with a venereal disease, provided that the other party is informed of the presence of the disease and there is a proportionately justifying cause for the marriage or its use, such as the avoidance of incontinence." [29]

Furthermore, *salvo meliore iudicio,* it seems unlikely that the Church will declare it to be against the natural law for victims of social disease to marry. For, if one consider the substance of marriage with respect to the consent of the parties and the transfer of mutual conjugal rights, in what way could the marriage of such persons be said to be contrary to the natural law by reason of their affliction? It is rather to be assumed that it would be against the natural law to deprive them of their innate right to contract marriage. The Church, however, could establish, within the limits that will presently be indicated, an absolute impediment that would take away from such a diseased person his innate right to marry. But it is only quite exceptionally and for the gravest reasons that the Church could make an absolute impediment by which a determinate class of persons would be forbidden to marry, or even through an invalidating law be rendered incapable of marrying.[30]

De Smet says that there are only two sufficiently grave reasons for recourse to this extraordinary procedure: "the necessity of defending the life and rights of a third person, and the necessity of defending and vindicating the common good of society." [31] The first reason exists in the case of a person afflicted with a communicable social disease if the Church for the protection of the spouse should forbid one so affected to marry as long as the danger of contagion is present.

---

[29] Moore and Connell, "Marriage and Venereal Infection."—*The Ecclesiastical Review,* C (1939), 332.

[30] This, of course, is a case apart from the one in which the prohibition or invalidation of marriage rests upon the spontaneous renunciation of the right on the part of one who takes a vow of chastity or of celibacy, or receives Sacred Orders. Cf. De Smet, *Betrothment and Marriage,* n. 423.

[31] *Loc. cit.*

To sum up the case for the authority of the State in this matter with respect to baptized persons, one must bear in mind several fundamental and important principles. The Church alone can declare to what extent the natural law prohibits or invalidates marriage for the baptized. If the State is to exercise over the baptized its power of enforcing the natural law, the exercise of that power must be limited to matters prescribed or forbidden by the natural law *according to the teachings of the Church.* Hence, if there is to be a civil law, applicable to all subjects of the State, for the purpose of counteracting the spread of social disease through marriage, such a law would have to be stated, as Connell suggests, in some such words as these: "Syphilitics may not marry unless the other party is forewarned and there is a justifying cause for the marriage, the Catholic Church being the judge in this matter." [32] Otherwise such legislation would lie outside the province of authority proper to the State.

The same principle is applicable in the event that the civil law is framed in such a manner as to delay marriage until a cure can be effected rather than directly to forbid it. Vermeersch presents the following query: "Admitting that the State has no right to forbid marriage permanently, can it forbid it temporarily to persons who, for a certain period, would be sources of infection to the persons they might marry?" The answer he gives is: "The State could exercise such power, at least by putting itself in agreement with the competent authority, which, in the case of baptized persons, is the Church." [33]

What is to be said of the right of the State to make these health laws for its unbaptized subjects? First of all it must be remembered that it is not certain that it is against the natural law for a person afflicted with a social disease to marry. Hence, it cannot be urged that the State by passing health laws is merely enforcing an obligation already incumbent upon that person from the natural law itself. But the State for its unbaptized subjects (just as

---

[32] "Compulsory Blood Tests before Marriage."—*The Ecclesiastical Review,* CI (1939), 28.

[33] Vermeersch, *What is Marriage?* (transl. by T. L. Bouscaren, New York: The America Press, 1932), n. 126.

the Church for the baptized) does have the power—subject to the same qualifications and restrictions as is the power of the Church in this matter—to deprive a person suffering from venereal infection of that innate right to marry which he is recognized as having by the natural law. This deprivation can be effected only for the protection of the spouse or for the common good, and for such time as may be required to eliminate the danger of contagion.[34]

Finally, it must be remembered that the lawmakers in our country would be more inclined to base their enactments on medical opinions and sociological considerations rather than on the teachings of theologians and canonists. Such notions as the innate right of a man to marry, the sacredness of marriage as a divine institution, the distinction between diriment and impedient impediments, and the difference between validity and licitness in relation to the marriage bond, are concepts which appear all too seldom to come within the ken of civil authorities, or which at best seem to become known to them only in a vague and confused way. Looking upon marriage as merely another civil contract; they legislate for it solely with a view to make certain things concerning marriage legal and certain things illegal, and they recognize almost no limitations on their lawmaking powers—least of all from what they may term "religious scruples."[35]

Hence, from the purely practical point of view, even a law framed in the manner suggested above would have little real significance for them, and would in all probability present great difficulties in its application through secular channels. Perhaps the best solution is to be found in a law which would require couples intending to be married to submit to a medical examination and each to be informed of the other's condition. But let the law

---

[34] This necessarily excludes any *purely eugenic* legislation, i.e., laws which are intended only to preclude the generation of defective or diseased offspring.

[35] Cf., e.g., Zollman, *American Church Law* (St. Paul: West Publishing Co., 1933), pp. 22-23, where it is stated: "Nor will the state by scruples claimed to be religious be prevented from enacting and enforcing proper police regulations. It may . . . require male persons making application for a marriage license to file a doctor's certificate with the county clerk certifying that they are free from acquired venereal diseases without trenching in the least upon religious liberty."

stop with that and require nothing further; it should not forbid them to marry if they still wish to do so despite the presence of a social disease. "Such a law . . . will be entirely within the competency of the state. Then, if a couple have a sufficient reason to marry, despite the presence of syphilis, they may do so according to the normal form prescribed by the Church. Thus will be preserved the exclusive rights of the Church to declare how far the natural law binds as regards marriage and to establish matrimonial impediments for the baptized." [36]

Article 2

Civil Impediments to Marriage

The general principles governing the authority of the Church to establish impediments for the baptized, and of the State to establish impediments for the unbaptized, have already been set forth.[37] Some impediments are common to both canonical and civil legislation; some are peculiar to the law of the Church; and others are to be found only in civil law. Although the first and third of these groups of impediments present most of the conflicts of jurisdiction, consideration will also have to be given to points of competence in the second group, particularly from the standpoint of the relations of Church and State. The various impediments will be treated in more or less detail according as the degree of conflict or the importance of relative competence may demand.

The first civil impediment to be considered is that of *infancy* or *nonage*. Though usually designated by these terms, it corresponds to the impediment of *aetas* in Church law. In civil law it is generally recognized that persons wishing to be married must be capable of giving intelligent matrimonial consent. At common law the age at which they are deemed capable of giving such consent is fourteen years for males and twelve years for females, but in most of the states this age of consent has been

---

[36] Connell, "Compulsory Blood Tests before Marriage."—*The Ecclesiastical Review,* CI (1939), 30.

[37] Cf. Chapter IV, *supra.*

raised by statute. Marriages contracted after the age of consent has been attained are generally regarded as valid, unless the permission of parents (in the case of minors) is required under penalty of nullity. Marriages contracted below the age of consent but after the age of seven years are variously termed as *voidable* or *inchoate* or *imperfect.*[38]

These *inchoate* marriages can, according to civil law, be declared void at the option either of the parties or of their parents, or they can be validated by cohabitation of the parties after the age of consent is reached. Marriages contracted before the age of seven are absolutely void in civil law. These regulations, like those of canon law, are radically founded in the natural law, which is directly concerned with the capacity to give true matrimonial consent and only indirectly with the age. Such laws of the State are binding on the unbaptized; and their marriages contracted in contravention of such an invalidating civil impediment of nonage are invalid. But for the baptized the Church will not regard their marriages as valid unless the male has completed the sixteenth year and the female the fourteenth year of age.[39]

If the civil law requires a higher age than that established by the Church, then for the baptized a compliance with such civil regulations cannot be demanded for the validity of their marriages. This would be true, too, according to the opinion of the majority of canonists, of marriages contracted between an infidel and a Christian, if the Christian had attained the requisite canonical age, and the infidel had attained the age of consent required by the natural law but had not yet reached the requisite civil age. The Church, however, urges pastors to dissuade the young from marrying before the age at which marriage is usually and customarily contracted in their respective countries.[40] But this obviously is a merely directive norm which touches neither upon

---

[38] Cf. Smith, *Handbook of Elementary Law* (2. ed., by A. H. McGray, St. Paul: West Publishing Co., 1939), 171; also Alford, *Ius Matrimoniale Comparatum*, n. 87.

[39] Canon 1067, §1.

[40] Canon 1067, §2.

the validity nor necessarily on the lawfulness of a contrary act on the part of the persons wishing to marry.

Finally, it is important to note one fundamental difference in the legislation of Church and State with regard to the marriages of those who are over seven years of age, but who have not yet attained the requisite canonical or civil age. As stated above, such marriages can under the civil law be validated by simple cohabitation of the parties as husband and wife; and this remains true despite the fact that the impediment of defect of age as it exists in civil law is, according to canonical terminology, a diriment impediment.[41] By canon law, on the other hand, if the parties had married before attaining the canonical age, the impediment ceases by lapse of time, but the marriage does not thereby become valid; the parties must renew their consent.[42]

Impotence is generally recognized in civil law either as an impediment which renders marriage void or voidable, or as a ground for a civil divorce *a vinculo*. The incapacity that it contemplates must exist at the time of the marriage and must be an incapacity to copulate; the element of fecundity does not enter into consideration.[43] By common law, impotence renders a marriage voidable; and in some states of the Union the impediment has that effect by statute. In one or two states the impediment of impotence renders a marriage absolutely void, so that a judicial process for a declaration of nullity of the marriage is not strictly required. But in most of the states antecedent and incurable impotence constitutes a ground for civil divorce, but is not regarded as a diriment impediment.[44]

Now, impotence is generally defined by theologians and canonists as "*impossibilitas perficiendi copulam coniugalem seu ac-*

---

[41] Cf. Alford, *Ius Matrimoniale Comparatum*, n. 87.

[42] Cf. canon 1133.

[43] Cf. Smith, *Handbook of Elementary Law*, 171.

Although the civil law and canon law are in accord in taking cognizance of the difference between impotence and sterility, yet it must be borne in mind that civil jurists do not consistently adhere to that distinction. Consequently, certain physical conditions that actually bring about impotence are, in civil law, regarded as producing sterility.

[44] Cf. Alford, *Ius Matrimoniale Comparatum*, n. 100.

tionem per se generationi aptam."[45] Thus it is characterized as an *impossibilitas coeundi* to distinguish it from sterility which is an *impossibilitas generandi.* From this definition it is evident that impotence is an impediment deriving from the natural law itself, since it militates against the object of the matrimonial consent and contravenes even the primary end of marriage. And, indeed, the canonical legislation takes cognizance of that fact when it decrees that "antecedent and perpetual impotence, either on the part of the man or on the part of the woman, whether known or unknown to the other party, and whether absolute or relative, invalidates marriage by the very law of nature."[46] This legislation, then, is not an enactment of a merely ecclesiastical law, but rather a definition or determination of the natural law, and consequently is binding on all persons whether baptized or unbaptized.[47]

Since the Church alone is competent to declare authentically in what cases the divine law forbids the contracting of marriage or nullifies the attempt to contract it,[48] therefore the right to establish or indicate the limits of this impediment does not belong to the civil authority. Of course it cannot be denied that the State has the power over her unbaptized subjects to enforce the natural law as such, or as authentically declared by the Church. But insofar as the civil authority attempts to introduce variations or changes into the determination of the natural law, such legislation is invalid because it is outside the sphere of secular competence.

In those states, therefore, where impotence is held to constitute a ground for divorce, the legislation in that respect is invalid. Apart from any question of the right of the State to dissolve the marriage bond, it is evident that the very term *divorce* presupposes a valid marriage. But if one of the parties was impotent, then there could not have been a valid marriage. Again, the term *voidable* not only signifies a marriage for which a declara-

[45] Payen, *De Matrimonio,* I, n. 983; cf. also Cappello, *De Sacramentis,* III, n. 342; Wernz, *Ius Matrimoniale,* n. 342.

[46] Canon 1068, §1.

[47] Cappello, *De Sacramentis,* III, n. 347, 5º; Alford, *Ius Matrimoniale Comparatum,* n. 98.

[48] Canon 1038, §1; cf. also *supra,* Chapter IV, p. 38.

tion of nullity may be obtained (provided that the nullity be established, for the marriage enjoys the favor of the law and is presumed to be valid), but also implies that the nullity of the marriage may be healed. This opens the way to false interpretations with regard to the impediment of impotence, for in some states there are established time limits (*fatalia legis*) for attacking the validity of the marriage. Moreover, in some states not only is the impotent party excluded from bringing judicial action, but, further, the party who is free of the impediment may by condonation lose the right to have the marriage declared null.[49] These notions are all contrary to the absolute nullity that results from the impediment of impotence.

In theory the civil impediment of *prior marriage* is the same as the impediment of *ligamen* in canon law, for, on the surface at least, it is recognized in civil law that a valid and undissolved prior marriage of either party renders a subsequent marriage absolutely void *ab initio,* and that bigamy is a crime punishable by law. But in fact and in practice the civil jurisprudence in regard to this impediment is vastly different from the canonical legislation. The very foundation of this difference lies in the failure of the State to admit the jurisdiction of the Church over marriage within its proper province of competence. For that reason if a marriage is declared null by competent ecclesiastical authority, such a declaration has absolutely no value according to civil law; and a person who had obtained that declaration and then attempted a second marriage without a divorce or declaration of nullity from the civil authority would be regarded as a bigamist. On the other hand, a person who had obtained a divorce and thereupon contracted a second marriage despite the fact that the first bond was valid by Church law would not commit bigamy under the civil law.

The civil impediment of prior marriage loses most of its real

---

[49] Cf. Alford, *Ius Matrimoniale Comparatum,* sectio 9, *passim.*

It must be noted that in civil law the term "voidable marriage" denotes a "void marriage" that is regarded as valid until the nullity is established by some juridical process. Hence, fundamentally the civil impediment of impotence is, if proved to exist in a particular case, a diriment impediment.

force and value because of the fact that by civil law a perfectly valid marriage, though it is ratified and consummated, can be dissolved by a civil divorce. Hence " the State denounces polygamy as contrary to the fundamental law of all Christian nations and punishes it as a great crime; but in practice, because it arrogates to itself the power of dissolving that which is indissoluble, it renders polygamy legitimate by its own laws." [50]

The impediment itself, in addition to being included among the diriment impediments in the Code of Canon Law,[51] is an impediment of the natural law and of the divine positive law, for it is rooted in the essential properties (the unity and indissolubility) of marriage, and it flows from the divine prohibition of polygamous unions.[52] As a declaration of the divine law, therefore, this canonical enactment binds the unbaptized as well as the baptized.

Some of the civil deviations and variations from that norm have already been pointed out. The legislation on this impediment is one outstanding example of the grave errors into which the State can be led, and of the indescribable harm that can be wrought upon souls, once the proper ordering of authority between Church and State is disregarded. The result has been not merely a denial of the rights of the Church. Far worse, it has brought about arbitrary and ill-considered judicial decisions and even positive enactments that are directly opposed to the divine law. For that reason it would be of little value to analyze at greater length the conflict of jurisdiction or the disputed points of competence in relation to this impediment. The rights are clearly defined: their proper exercise is swallowed up in the extravagant claims of a usurped power which is utterly devoid of the authority to which it pretends.

The impediment of *consanguinity* as found in civil law offers several difficulties of presentation. Because of the many variations and differences among the laws of the separate states, a comprehensive examination of the legislation would be beyond the im-

---

[50] Alford, *Ius Matrimoniale Comparatum,* n. 114. Cf. also sectio 10, *passim;* Wernz, *Ius Matrimoniale,* n. 372; Cappello, *De Sacramentis,* III, n. 409.

[51] Canon 1069, §1.

[52] Cf. Wernz, *Ius Matrimoniale,* n. 361; Payen, *De Matrimonio,* I, n. 1047.

mediate purposes of the present study. Moreover, any comparison between the civil and the canonical legislation is made more complex by reason of the fact that the civil statutes designate by name (as: brother, sister, etc.) the relationships that constitute the impediment, whereas the Code of Canon Law sets forth rather the degrees of relationship within which marriage is forbidden. To avoid a tedious and lengthy presentation of the subject, the impediment will first be described as set forth in the Code, and thereupon the exact degree of its correspondence with the natural law will be observed. From that mode of procedure the binding force of this impediment on the baptized and the unbaptized, and the competence of the Church and the State, can then be determined.

It is stated in the Code of Canon Law: " In the direct line marriage is invalid between all ascendants and descendants whether legitimate or illegitimate. In the collateral line marriage is invalid to the third degree inclusive, but the impediment is multiplied only when the common stock is multiplied. Marriage is never allowed if there is a doubt whether the parties are related in some degree of the direct line or in the first degree of the collateral line." [53]

Marriage between blood-relatives in the first degree of the direct line is in the opinion of all considered as *certainly* invalid by the natural law. Marriage between blood-relatives in the other degrees of the direct line is in the more prevalent and tenable opinion likewise considered invalid by the natural law, so that the invalidity of such a marriage derives more probably from the natural law than from merely human legislation.[54] Marriage between blood-relatives in the first degree of the collateral line is in the more prevalent and tenable opinion regarded as invalid in consequence of the secondary precepts of the natural law, so that the invalidity of the marriage derives more probably from these secondary precepts than merely from ecclesiastical law.

---

[53] Canon 1076.

[54] Wernz, *Ius Matrimoniale,* n. 410; Wernz-Vidal, *Ius Matrimoniale,* n. 347; Cappello, *De Sacramentis,* III, n. 518; De Smet, *Betrothment and Marriage,* n. 607; Payen, *De Matrimonio,* I, n. 1440.

Marriage between blood-relatives in other degrees of the collateral line is universally considered as *certainly* not invalid in consequence of any divine law, natural or positive.[55]

Thus the impediment in the collateral line with respect to degrees beyond the first (but only up to and including the third) is *certainly* a merely ecclesiastical law, and therefore is binding only on the baptized. For the baptized the impediment of consanguinity renders null a marriage within any of the degrees listed by the canon, unless, of course, a dispensation be obtained for those degrees of relationship over which the Church has the power to dispense. Moreover, if Christians obtain from the competent ecclesiastical authority a dispensation from the impediment within a certain degree, their marriage will be valid notwithstanding a civil prohibition against marriage of persons related in that degree. For the unbaptized, however, the legislation of their respective states is valid and binding. As a result, in the absence of any civil provisions in the matter, the only degree of consanguinity within which the marriage of infidels would be certainly invalid is the first degree of the direct line, for it is not incontestably certain that marriage within any other degrees, whether direct or indirect, is rendered null and void by the very law of nature.

Since the promulgation of the Code of Canon Law the civil and the canonical legislation on the impediment of *affinity* have generally and theoretically been in harmony in decreeing that the impediment arises only from a valid marriage and not from mere carnal intercourse.[56] In Church law the impediment is recognized as being of its nature perpetual, so that it does not cease by the death of a spouse, or by the dissolution through Apostolic dispensation of the bond of a ratified and non-consummated marriage, or by the dissolution of the marriage through solemn religious profession. In civil law, although this quality of permanence is generally recognized, so that the impediment remains after the dissolution of the bond by the death of one of the

[55] Cf. the same authors for a thorough exposition of the arguments used and the authorities cited to support these conclusions.

[56] Cf. Canons 97 and 1077; Alford, *Ius Matrimoniale Comparatum*, n. 151,

parties or after the obtaining of a civil divorce, yet in many states of this country the established jurisprudence does not seem to admit this permanence.[57] Obviously, the practical effect of such an interpretation is that in those states there is no impediment of affinity which strictly can be regarded as such.

Another practical difference in the secular and the ecclesiastical dispositions derives from this fact: In canon law it seems that the impediment arises only from a ratified marriage (*matrimonium ratum*), but not from a merely legitimate marriage (*matrimonium legitimum*), i.e., a marriage validly contracted between two unbaptized persons,[58] whereas by civil law the impediment arises from any valid marriage, though here, too, the word *valid* will have to be understood as meaning valid in the eyes of the civil law. But at all events the canonical impediment of affinity is generally held by theologians and canonists to be an impediment of the ecclesiastical law alone, and in no degree and in neither line to be derived from the natural or divine positive

---

[57] Cf. Alford, *Ius Matrimoniale Comparatum,* sectio 12, *passim.*

[58] This question is controverted among canonists; the dispute arises over the meaning to be attached to the term *rato tantum* in canon 97. Among those who hold that the impediment arises also in valid marriages of the unbaptized may be mentioned: Wernz-Vidal, *Ius Matrimoniale,* nn. 360 and 367; Vlaming, *Praelectiones Iuris Matrimonialis,* I, n. 353; and Gasparri, *De Matrimonio,* n. 715. The opinion that the impediment does not arise in such marriages is held by: Cappello, *De Sacramentis,* III, n. 538; De Smet, *Betrothment and Marriage,* n. 613; and Payen, *De Matrimonio,* I, n. 1485.

According to canon 1015, §1, a *matrimonium ratum* refers only to the sacramental union of two baptized persons. Since the term is explicitly defined there, it is to be presumed that the legislator meant in canon 97 to use the term *ratum* in its strict juridical sense. Therefore, it being practically certain that only the marriage of two baptized parties is a *matrimonium ratum,* the opinion which restricts the foundation of the impediment of affinity to the marriage of two baptized persons seems at present more probable than the others. There is, moreover, a *dubium iuris* whether affinity arises from any marriage other than that of two baptized persons. Pending an interpretation of the Holy See on this point, one may apply canon 15; hence, in practice, the impediment springs only from a valid marriage of two baptized persons, and, accordingly, does not arise either from a *matrimonium legitimum* or from a marriage between a baptized person and an unbaptized person.

law.[59] If, then, there be no impediment established by civil law, marriage among unbaptized persons related by affinity will be valid; but if an unbaptized person wished to marry a baptized person related to him by affinity as a result of a previous ratified marriage, then the unbaptized person would be indirectly subject to the ecclesiastical impediment of affinity.

The State is competent to legislate for infidels with regard to this impediment, and the marriages of these persons are subject to any invalidating effects of the civil provisions. Certainly the State has no *right* to make such laws for her baptized subjects; but *de facto* these regulations are made civilly binding on all citizens, Christians and infidels alike. In order, therefore, to avoid the grave harm to himself and his intended spouse, a Catholic who could obtain a dispensation from the canonical impediment might yet have to submit to the civil restriction—certainly not by virtue of the civil law itself, but only out of charity, for generally the marriages contracted within the forbidden degrees of affinity (as well as of consanguinity) are regarded as incestuous unions.[60] The parties, moreover, are guilty of a criminal offense and are liable to the statutory punishment for a crime of that nature.

Of all the matrimonial impediments the one arising from *legal relationship* presents the least conflict of jurisdiction between Church and State. The Church has "canonized" the civil regulations on this matter by decreeing that if by the civil law legal relationship, arising from adoption, renders marriage either unlawful or invalid, the marriage is likewise either unlawful or invalid in canon law.[61] In the United States, however, this impediment does not exist among the marriage laws of the various states, but it is established as a diriment impediment in the civil code of the Territory of Puerto Rico.[62]

It should be remarked that the constituent elements of adoption, as well as the existence, scope, nature, and duration of the impedi-

[59] Cf., e.g., Wernz, *Ius Matrimoniale,* n. 430; Merkelbach, *Summa Theologiae Moralis,* III, n. 913.

[60] Cf. Robinson, *Elementary Law* (Revised ed., Boston, 1910), n. 505.

[61] Canons 1059 and 1079.

[62] Cf. Alford, *Ius Matrimoniale Comparatum,* n. 163.

ment of legal relationship, are to be determined from the civil law. But in matrimonial causes of the baptized (and this holds true even if only one of the parties is baptized) the interpretation of the impediment in relation to a particular marriage would obviously pertain to the ecclesiastical tribunal. And, finally, it should be noted that the impediment of legal relationship, even though based on the civil dispositions in those places where it exists, is formally a canonical impediment. Consequently, for the baptized a dispensation would have to be obtained from the Church and not from the State; and, conversely, a dispensation granted by the civil authority would not remove the impediment for Christians.[63] If, moreover, there is question of the intermarriage of a baptized person and an unbaptized person, and the State has granted to the unbaptized party a dispensation from the civil impediment of legal relationship, the baptized party must still obtain from the Church a dispensation from the canonical impediment. This, again, follows logically from the fact that for the baptized the civil law provides only the material element of the impediment, whereas the Church law gives to legal relationship its real form as a canonical impediment.

Among the matrimonial impediments may be considered that of *insanity,* although strictly regarded the lack of reason as an obstacle to marriage is based on a defect of consent and may therefore be termed an impediment only in a broad sense. The civil legislation varies among the different states, but by the common law insanity is regarded as an impediment that renders marriage absolutely void. To that extent the civil law is, in a general way, in harmony with the canonical provisions on the matter. The Code, however, does not contain a specific canon in relation to insanity. The principle governing such cases is: " Marriage is constituted by the legitimately manifested consent of persons who are able by law to marry; and this consent cannot be supplied by any human power." [64]

Now, it is recognized that one of the obstacles to valid consent is insanity. But to be an obstacle in the sense of a diriment im-

---

[63] Cf. Wernz-Vidal, *Ius Matrimoniale,* n. 196.

[64] Canon 1081, §1.

pediment the insanity must at the moment of the celebration of the marriage be such as to leave the contracting party without a sufficient use of reason for the understanding of the substance of marriage.[65] Hence, considered purely from the viewpoint of its absolute invalidating effect, it does not matter whether the insanity is habitual or temporary, total or partial; what is important is whether the party was deprived of the sufficient use of reason at the very moment of marriage. Certainly, however, from the practical point of view attention must be given to these elements of permanence and extent, for in relation to the habitually insane the presumption is against a lucid interval, whereas, if the lack of reason is not continuous, marriage contracted at a supposed lucid interval would enjoy the favor of the law. The exact influence of the mental disability upon the human act requisite in the actual contracting of marriage must be determined in particular cases. To aid in this determination canonists have elaborated certain general principles regarding various states of insanity and their effects on the judgment and freedom which are essential to the very nature of the matrimonial contract.[66]

The Church, of course, does not encourage marriage on the part of a person afflicted with a mental disability, but she insists that the right to marry which such a person has from the natural law cannot be denied him absolutely; and if he contracts marriage at a moment when he is capable of giving valid consent his marriage must be recognized as valid. Therefore, only those persons who are so devoid of the use of reason, either habitually or actually (at the time of entering into the marital contract), that they have no understanding of the substance of the marriage contract, can be said to be incapacitated by the natural law itself for the contracting of marriage.[67] These fundamental concepts one must

---

[65] Cf. De Smet, *Betrothment and Marriage*, n. 533.

[66] Cf. e.g., Cappello, *De Sacramentis*, III, nn. 579-580; Pfatschbacher, *Eugenische Ehehindernisse*, eine kirchenrechtliche Studie, Theologische Studien der Österreichischen Leo-Gesellschaft, herausgegeben von Dr. Leopold Krebs und Dr. Josef Lehner, n. 34 (Wien: Verlag Mayer und Comp., 1933), 70-74.

[67] Cf. Wernz, *Ius Matrimoniale*, n. 41.

bear in mind in order rightly to evaluate the civil prescriptions in regard to insanity as an impediment to marriage.

The State, as has already been noted, is competent to legislate for the unbaptized in such matters, and as long as her laws do not go contrary to the norm of the natural law they are valid for and binding on the unbaptized. But the tendency in civil jurisprudence seems to be in the direction of widening the scope of this impediment in such a way as to forbid marriage to the feeble-minded, and that only for purely eugenic reasons, i.e., to prevent the generation of feeble-minded offspring. To this end marriage is either forbidden to such persons absolutely, or it is allowed them only if they first undergo an operation for sterilization. Regulations of such a kind obviously militate against the natural law itself, and certainly cannot find legitimate sanction.

Civil legislation in regard to insanity has followed a false course in another direction by providing that a civil divorce may be obtained on the ground of insanity—whether it existed at the time of the marriage or whether it developed at a later date. If the party was really insane at the time of the marriage, there could have been no bond to be "dissolved" by divorce; if the insanity developed later, it has no effect on the matrimonial contract itself—which, at all events, the State has no power to dissolve.

Drunkenness is likewise established in civil law as capable of having an invalidating effect on marriage. In canon law it is not reckoned among the impediments to marriage, but is usually treated by canonists among the other defects of consent based on the want of sufficient reason. When the drunkenness is such as to take away all use of reason it is equivalent to temporary insanity. It then renders the marriage invalid because the drunken person was incapable of giving a valid consent. But if the drunkenness is incomplete or only partial, then it does not render the marriage invalid.[68]

In this country the civil jurisprudence recognizes these same principles in that the marriage is judged to be valid or invalid according as the drunken party had or had not the use of sufficient

[68] Cf. Wernz-Vidal, *Ius Matrimoniale*, n. 456.

reason at the time the marriage was contracted.[69] In some few states, moreover, habitual drunkenness is an impedient impediment, and it is forbidden to grant a license to an habitual drunkard even though he be sober at the time. Inasmuch as these laws contemplate the avoidance of harm to the family and to society, they can rightfully be sanctioned in their enactment. But the State could not attach to these laws an invalidating effect, for such a disposition of the civil law would be contrary to the natural law.[70]

Of a nature similar to the laws forbidding the marriage of habitual drunkards are the civil provisions of a few states which prohibit the marriage of *habitual criminals*. For these laws it may also be said that they are prudent and proper insofar as they are intended to prevent harm to the family or to protect the common good. But certainly it would be wrong, in the case either of habitual drunkards or of habitual criminals, to go to the extent of establishing compulsory sterilization as a means of carrying out these civil prescriptions. Such a procedure is based not on any conceivable principle of just punishment for a crime committed, but solely on eugenic considerations which have usurped the rightful place of the aims of a higher order. That such a practice is morally wrong is clearly indicated by Pope Pius XI in his Encyclical on Christian Marriage.[71]

The question of *disease* as a civil impediment to marriage has been discussed at length in the article on the prerequisites for marriage.[72] A word more should be added here in regard to

---

[69] Alford, *Ius Matrimoniale Comparatum*, n. 220.

[70] *Ibidem*, n. 221.

[71] Ep. encycl. *Casti Connubii*—*AAS*, XXII (1930), 564-565.

The Holy Office, on March 21, 1931, was asked: "What is to be thought of the so-called 'Eugenic' theory, whether 'positive' or 'negative,' and of the means which it proposes for the improvement of human progeny, in disregard of the laws, natural, divine, or ecclesiastical, pertaining to marriage and the rights of individuals?" The reply was: "That theory is to be absolutely disapproved, held as false, and condemned, as is declared in the Encyclical on Christian Marriage of December 31, 1930."—*AAS*, XXIII (1931), 118; English translation from Bouscaren, *The Canon Law Digest* (2 vols., Milwaukee: Bruce, 1934–1943), I, 677–678.

[72] Cf. *supra*, pp. 62–70.

epilepsy, since many states have either made that an impediment to marriage, or permit epileptics to marry, but only if the woman is over forty-five years of age, or only if the afflicted party will submit to an operation for sterilization.[73] The eugenic tendencies in the two latter prescriptions are evident. Such legislation cannot be justified. To establish epilepsy as an absolute impediment would be to forbid marriage absolutely to a person who is fit by the natural law to contract marriage. This, as already indicated in the previous discussion of health laws, the State cannot do.

An often discussed question in regard to marriage is that of the advisability of marriage between members of different races. From the biological standpoint, it is asserted by some that a mixture of races produces inferior offspring; by others it is claimed that no solid physiological proof can be brought to support that theory. From the sociological standpoint, it is maintained by some that the common good of society requires that interracial marriages be discouraged because of the social dissensions and difficulties arising from them; by others it is held that such a view is based on specious reasoning and that the real purpose behind these attempts to forbid such marriages is to protect and maintain the social, political, and economic supremacy of one race. Whatever be the merit of these various opinions, it is a fact that in more than half of the states of this country there are in force laws which forbid marriage between a person of the Caucasian race and a person of non-Caucasian origin.[74]

With regard to the unbaptized the State has the power to establish impediments for them when they marry among themselves. Hence there seems to be no reason which bars the State from setting up *racial difference* as a diriment impediment for the marriages of her infidel subjects. By such laws the civil authority is not going contrary to the natural law, for they do not take away altogether the right of the person to marry, but rather place a certain restriction on that right.[75] This restriction is justified by

[73] Cf. Alford, *Ius Matrimoniale Comparatum*, n. 212.

[74] According to Alford (*Ius Matrimoniale Comparatum*, n. 201) there are laws of this kind in thirty of the United States.

[75] Nau, however, maintains that the justice and reasonableness of these laws may be questioned.—*Marriage Laws of the Code*, n. 9.

some authors on the ground that the prevailing prejudice ostracizes the parties who enter upon an interracial marriage, and that this social ostracism places a strain on the family relations by jeopardizing the mutual love and respect of the spouses.[76]

There is little reference to the question in the writings of Catholic theologians in this country. But Gilligan (who is among those who justify this restriction) draws an argument *a pari* from the attitude of older theologians towards marriage between a noble and a peasant.[77] It was admitted, he says, that there was nothing inherently wrong in such marriages, but because of the grave probability of quarrels, and also because of the shame of the relatives, theologians taught that such a marriage was illicit and in some cases sinful. Gilligan is of the opinion that the presumption of an interracial marriage coming to an unhappy end in this country is so strong that young people would sin against prudence if they deliberately entered into such a union. However, it is not certain that these marriages would be sinful. Hence, as regards the baptized (and particularly Catholics), although the civil prohibition against interracial marriage would not as a law be binding on them, it must be said that " prudence and the good of the couples themselves would induce a pastor to dissuade in most cases such interracial marriages . . . however, this would not justify a pastor to refuse to assist at such a Catholic marriage." [78]

The very nature of the marriage contract as involving a transfer of mutual rights demands that there be expressed the marital consent of two determinate persons. Hence a substantial error in regard to the person vitiates the consent and renders the marriage invalid by the natural law itself.[79] By the natural law, too, error in regard to the quality of a person when it is equivalent to sub-

[76] Cf. Alford, *Ius Matrimoniale Comparatum*, n. 208; La Farge, *The Race Question and the Negro* (New York: Longmans, Green & Co., 1943), 195–198.

[77] " The Color Line Considered Morally."—*The Ecclesiastical Review*, LXXXI (1929), 482 ff.

[78] Nau, *Marriage Laws of the Code*, n. 9.

[79] Wernz-Vidal, *Ius Matrimoniale*, n. 467; De Smet, *Betrothment and Marriage*, n. 524; cf. also canon 1083, §1.

stantial error about the very person likewise renders marriage null because of the lack of mutual consent.[80] These two classes of error, since they place an obstacle to the matrimonial consent required by the law of nature, render null the marriages not only of the baptized but also of the unbaptized (even apart from any provisions of the civil law). In this country, although only one state has it established by law that *error* concerning the person nullifies marriage, nevertheless from general principles in regard to consent the diriment effects of such error are everywhere recognized.[81]

In the law of the Church it is decreed that error in regard to the quality of a person invalidates the marriage contract only if it be an error about the servile condition of the person.[82] Now, this disposition of the canon is of ecclesiastical law only, and hence is binding only on the baptized. In civil law there exist numerous provisions concerning error of quality, and most of these are determined by the principles governing *fraud* as it affects the marriage contract. Generally, these civil regulations are, acording to Alford, " broader and less strict than the discipline of canon law, but it does not seem that they are contrary to the natural law." [83]

Discussing the power of the State to make such laws, Alford points out that although in fact the Church has not wished to do so nevertheless she could further extend the diriment effect of error of quality as an impediment of ecclesiastical law.[84] Hence, he concludes, " it seems that there are not lacking reasons which enable the state reasonably to declare marriages of infidels entered into under the influence of substantial fraud to be invalid, provided that such laws are reasonable and proper and do not

---

[80] Wernz-Vidal, *op. cit.*, n. 468; canon 1083, §2, 1º.

[81] Alford, *Ius Matrimoniale Comparatum*, n. 187.

[82] Canon 1083, §2, 2º. This, of course, is in addition to the declaration regarding error about quality when it is tantamount to substantial error about the very person. That aspect has already been discussed above.

[83] *Ius Matrimoniale Comparatum*, n. 188.

[84] The Church is unwilling to do this, says Cappello, " ne innumera oriantur dubia et quaestiones circa validitatem matrimoniorum, cum publico et gravi animarum damno."—*De Sacramentis*, III, n. 585.

attempt to render the matrimonial contract merely rescindible." [85] But certainly wherever these laws are so lax as to admit of all kinds of abuse they lose that necessary foundation of reasonableness and propriety and cannot be sanctioned; and wherever they provide that marriage contracted under the influence of fraud is rescindible, these civil laws are contrary to the divine law.

Finally, a brief consideration must be given to *violence or fear* as constituting in civil law a diriment impediment to marriage. Once again, because of the complexity of the subject and because of the diverse application of these elements among the laws and judicial decisions of the various states, it will be helpful to set forth first the canonical discipline. From that, then, can be determined the exact competence of the civil authority in legislating on the matter for its unbaptized subjects.

The Code states that a marriage is null if contracted because of violence or grave fear arising from an extrinsic source and unjustly inflicted, to free himself from which the person is compelled to choose marriage; but no other fear, even though it give cause to the contract, entails the nullity of marriage.[86] It is certain that, if the inflicted physical violence be so strong or the induced fear be so grave as to take away absolutely the voluntary character of the act posited by the person subjected to such duress, under these circumstances the required marital consent cannot be given and therefore the marriage is invalid by the natural law itself.[87] Consequently, marriages of the unbaptized contracted under the constraint of such violence or fear would be invalid whether or not there existed any positive civil determination on the matter. But when there is question of moral force or fear by which the voluntary nature of the act of giving consent is greatly lessened but not destroyed, though it is certain that the marriage is nullified by ecclesiastical law, it is controverted whether the marriage is invalid by the natural law also.[88]

---

[85] Alford, *Ius Matrimoniale Comparatum,* n. 188.

[86] Canon 1087.

[87] Cf. Wernz, *Ius Matrimoniale,* n. 267; Cappello, *De Sacramentis,* III, n. 606; De Smet, *Betrothment and Marriage,* n. 535.

[88] That the invalidation arises from the natural law (and this seems to be the more probable opinion) is held, among others, by Wernz (*Ius Matri-*

In these circumstances, then, only the marriages of Christians (who alone are bound by the purely canonical dispositions) are certainly invalid. It is not incontestably certain that in similar circumstances the marriages contracted by unbaptized parties are invalid, for it is not above all doubt that such parties are bound by the impediment of violence and fear as promulgated in Church law, since it remains an open question whether the Church law enlarges upon the demand of the natural law itself. For infidels, the civil law to which they are subject will determine the status of their marriages contracted under the influence of violence and fear. In the absence of any civil provision on the matter, their marriages in the face of this doubt of law are to be regarded as valid according to the norm of canon 1014, unless, in the case of one converted to the Faith, there should be occasion for the application of canon 1127.[89]

Article 3

Civil Provisions in Regard to the Celebration of Marriage

The essence of the matrimonial contract, when it is actually made (*matrimonium in fieri*), consists in the mutual consent of the parties, whereby they mutually give and accept the perpetual and exclusive right to the use of those bodily functions which in and of themselves are suited for the procreation of children.[90] This consent, which in itself is an act of the will, must be externally manifested in some way. The circumstances or conditions attendant upon this manifestation, as also the various means by which this matrimonial consent is legitimately manifested, make up the *form* for the celebration of marriage. It is not a question here of the theological concept of the form (as distinguished

---

moniale, n. 266) and Cappello (*De Sacramentis*, III, n. 609). The opinion that such a marriage is null only by ecclesiastical law is held by De Smet (*Betrothment and Marriage*, n. 535) and Gasparri (*De Matrimonio*, nn. 839-842).

[89] Cf. Alford, *Ius Matrimoniale Comparatum*, n. 173; Cappello, *De Sacramentis*, III, n. 610.

[90] Canon 1081; cf. also Merkelbach, *Summa Theologiae Moralis*, III, n. 773.

from the matter) of the sacrament of matrimony, which would pertain only to the marriages of Christians. Rather, it is a matter of the juridical or substantial form that is required for the validity of the marital contract, whether the marriage be among Christians or among infidels. This juridical form may be distinguished as the merely *natural form,* i.e., the form which is sufficient by the natural law, the *canonical form,* which is prescribed by Church law, and the *civil form,* which is required by secular legislation.

So far as the natural law is concerned no special formality is demanded; all that is required of the parties capable of contracting marriage is a mutual consent externally and reciprocally manifested by words or by signs or in any other manner.[91] This form as required by the natural law is sufficient for the validity of the marriages among the unbaptized, not only in places where there is no civil disposition regarding the formalities for the celebration of marriage, but also in places where the civil formalities are prescribed as a requirement of lawfulness only. This simple form of the natural law is sufficient also for the validity of marriages among those baptized persons who are not bound to observe the canonical form.

The Church alone is competent to legislate in this matter for the baptized, and if she sees fit to exempt certain persons from the observance of the form prescribed by her law (as in fact she does in canon 1099, §2), then those persons are not bound by any form other than that required by the natural law. They are not bound to observe the formalities prescribed by civil law (even those required for validity), because the civil authority has not the power to legislate for the marriages of the baptized, except as regards the merely civil effects of such marriages.[92] Hence, a common law marriage between baptized non-Catholics would be valid even though the civil law of the place did not recognize the validity of such a union.[93] On the other hand, it

91 De Smet, *Betrothment and Marriage,* n. 103; Cappello, *De Sacramentis,* III, n. 648.

92 Cf. Chapter IV, *supra.*

93 Cf. Dillon, *Common Law Marriage,* 61.

cannot be said that the validity of their marriages as to form (or in any other respect) is to be determined by the regulations of the heretical or schismatical sects to which they may belong, for these non-Catholic religious bodies lack any authority in such matters. By divine law the sole authority by which the marriages of Christians are governed is the Catholic Church.[94]

The merely *natural form* is sufficient also for the validity of a marriage between an unbaptized person and a baptized person who is not held to the canonical form of marriage. In such a case the matter of the form of marriage, according to the more probable opinion, is governed not by the civil law but by the law of the Church. But since no formality is demanded by the Church in this instance, the civil prescriptions regarding the form cannot affect the validity of the marriage.[95]

The principles concerning the canonical form of marriage are set forth in the Code in canons 1094–1098 and 1102. Without going into these in detail, one may here state that ordinarily it is required that the marriage be celebrated before a competent priest and in the presence of two witnesses; provision, however, is made for the celebration of marriage without the assistance of a priest in certain extraordinary cases. And canon 1099 states who are bound by the canonical form and who are exempt from its observance.

As regards the civil form for marriage, it must be said that the State is fully competent to legislate in this matter for her unbaptized subjects when they marry among themselves. In prescribing the formalities for the celebration of marriage the civil authority may insist upon their observance under pain of nullity. For that reason, if two unbaptized persons should enter a common law marriage in a state where such unions are held by law

---

[94] Alford, *Ius Matrimoniale Comparatum,* n. 332; Cappello, *De Sacramentis,* III, n. 648. Cf. Leo XIII, ep. encycl. *Arcanum Divinae,* 10 feb. 1880, §§9 and 11—*Fontes,* n. 580; Pius XI, ep. encycl. *Casti Connubii—AAS,* XXII (1930), 539 and 589.

[95] This follows from what was said in Chapter IV, *supra,* concerning the competent authority over the marriage between a Christian and an infidel. For the application of the principles in this particular matter, cf. Alford, *Ius Matrimoniale Comparatum,* n. 334.

to be null, their marriage would be invalid.[96] In this country the form required by civil law for the celebration of marriage differs among the various states, but generally there is prescribed some kind of ceremony before a civil official or a minister of religion.[97] There remain to be considered briefly some of the specific civil provisions in regard to the celebration of marriage, especially in regard to the minister, the witnesses, and the registration of the marriage after the ceremony.

From the viewpoint of the sacrament of Christian marriage, the parties to the contract are themselves the ministers of the sacrament. But in reference to marriage in general (both among Christians and among infidels), the term *minister* is often used in a broad sense to designate the priest, minister, rabbi, or civil official who may be competent to assist or officiate at the celebration of the marriage. It is in this broad sense that the term is used here. In the United States the principle of religious liberty has been given expression by the recognition of all forms of religion as being equal in the eyes of the State. Consequently, all licensed or ordained " ministers of the Gospel " (and this term either by statute or by accepted jurisprudence includes priests and rabbis as well as Protestant ministers) are generally designated by the laws of the various states as competent to officiate at marriage ceremonies. In two states of the Union ministers of religion exclusively are held to be competent to assist at marriages; but in all others this competence is extended to certain civil officials. In no state, however, is there required a civil ceremony apart from the religious ceremony.[98]

The parties are free to choose whether they will contract marriage before a minister of religion or before a competent civil official; or, if they wish, the parties may have both a religious and a civil ceremony. The attitude of the civil authority on this point may be said to be a favorable one in that it places no positive obstacles to or restrictions on the exercise of the sacerdotal func-

96 Cf. Dillon, *Common Law Marriage,* 76.

97 Alford, *Ius Matrimoniale Comparatum,* n. 333.

98 The situation is quite different in Europe where in several countries a separate civil ceremony is demanded by law.

tion in assistance at marriage. In a certain sense, however, this attitude is a patronizing one, and from it there can arise certain practical conflicts of jurisdiction between Church and State. From the viewpoint of the State its own civil form is entirely sufficient for the validity of marriage between any two parties, baptized or unbaptized, who are capable of entering the marital relationship. Hence, a marriage between two Catholics contracted before a civil official or a Protestant minister would be held valid in civil law, whereas in fact such a marriage is invalid because of the lack of a properly observed canonical form. On the other hand, if the presence of a competent minister were demanded by civil law under pain of nullity, and if for some reason civil competence were denied a priest authorized by canon law to assist at the ceremony, the marriage of two Catholics, even though valid by the canonical form, could be regarded as invalid at civil law. In either case the civil authority would exceed its competence in attempting to apply its legislation to a matter over which it has no power.[99]

There is no practical difficulty arising from the civil requirements in this country for witnesses to the celebration of marriage. In almost half of the states there are no regulations on the matter; and in those states which directly or indirectly do require that marriage be celebrated in the presence of witnesses, neither the absence nor the incompetence of witnesses is regarded as having any effect on the validity of the marriage.[100] Here, again, there is a possibility of conflict of jurisdiction by reason of the failure of the State to recognize the binding force of the canonical form for those whom the Church holds to its observance, for by the law of the Church the presence of witnesses is required for the validity of the marriage.

In the discussion of the civil prerequisites for marriage it was pointed out that the granting of a marriage license or certificate

---

[99] For a more detailed presentation on the civil provisions of the various states in this country concerning competent and incompetent ministers for the celebration of marriage, cf. Alford, *Ius Matrimoniale Comparatum,* sectiones 34 and 38, *passim.*

[100] Alford, *Ius Matrimoniale Comparatum,* n. 367.

is usually the first step in the civil registration of the marriage.[101] This process of registration is customarily completed by the filing with the proper civil official of some formal notification that the ceremony has actually been performed. In order to establish a public record of the fact for the purpose of according recognition to the purely civil effects of marriage, the State is acting within its own province of authority when it enacts such requirements for all marriages. Wherefore, in commenting on the right of the State to demand that all marriages contracted be registered civilly, Nau rightly says: "It is a conscientious duty incumbent upon the officiating priest to make an official return to the State if the civil law so demands. Neglect in this matter can cause serious harm to the parties and to their children." [102]

The State may require that this registration be made within a definitely prescribed time after the marriage is contracted; and for failure to comply with the regulation she can impose a penalty on the contracting parties—but not on the officiating priest. This penalty may justly go so far as to concede the merely civil effects to the marriage only from the actual time that it is duly registered on the civil records; but it could not go so far as to deny to the bond, until the time of such registration, its status of validity or lawfulness, nor even so far as to withhold civil recognition to the inseparable effects of a marriage legitimately contracted in the eyes of the Church.[103]

Article 4

Civil Dispositions Regarding Separation, Divorce, and Declaration of Nullity

A—Separation of the Parties or Discontinuance of Cohabitation

The essence of marriage after the contract has been entered upon (*matrimonium in facto esse*) consists of that bond of the moral order which arises from the contract and is of itself per-

[101] Cf. *supra*, p. 58.

[102] *Marriage Laws of the Code*, n. 11.

[103] Ottaviani, *Institutiones Iuris Publici Ecclesiastici*, II, n. 337.

manent, i.e., the matrimonial bond. Upon this bond is based the state of life lived together and in common as husband and wife.[104] Married persons are, therefore, bound to live their conjugal life in common unless some just reason excuses them from doing so.[105]

Common conjugal life (i.e., community of bed, board, and dwelling), though it is required by the very nature of marriage, pertains rather to the integrity of marriage than directly to its substance. Hence, there may be just causes which will permit the consorts to discontinue cohabitation, *while the matrimonial bond itself remains undissolved.*[106] That there can be such legitimate reasons for the discontinuance of conjugal life is expressly asserted in Sacred Scripture,[107] and is sanctioned also in the teaching of the Church.[108]

The Code of Canon Law in canons 1128–1132 treats of the separation of husband and wife. After stating that separation is allowed for a just reason, the Code then lists some legitimate causes for separation and indicates certain conditions and restrictions for the exercise of the right to separate, and finally makes provision for the custody and education of the children. The whole tenor of the attitude and legislation of the Church on this question is perhaps best expressed in the words of Pope Leo XIII: " When, indeed, matters have come to such a pitch that it seems impossible for them [scil. husband and wife] to live together any longer, then the Church allows them to live apart, and strives at the same time to soften the evils of this separation by such remedies and helps as are suited to their condition; yet she never ceases to endeavor to bring about a reconciliation, and never despairs of doing so. But these are extreme cases; and they would seldom exist if men and women entered into the married state with proper dispositions . . ." [109]

[104] Cf. Merkelbach, *Summa Theologiae Moralis,* III, n. 776.

[105] Canon 1128.

[106] Cf. Petrovits, *The New Church Law on Matrimony* (2. ed., Philadelphia: McVey, 1926), n. 580.

[107] Matthew, 5:32 and 19:9; I Corinthians, 7:11.

[108] Conc. Trident., sess. xxiv, *de matrimonio,* can. 8; cf. also Leo XIII, ep. encycl., *Arcanum Divinae,* 10 feb. 1880, §25—*Fontes,* n. 580.

[109] Ep. encycl. *Arcanum Divinae,* §25—*Fontes,* n. 580; *The Pope and the People,* 42.

Apart from any consideration in detail of the canonical regulations on the separation of spouses, it should nevertheless be noted that the only intrinsic cause that justifies a *permanent* separation is adultery.[110] Certain other causes which are extrinsic to marriage are sufficient however to justify a *temporary* separation. (Among the partial list of such causes enumerated in the Code are apostasy, a criminal manner of living, cruelty, grave spiritual or corporal danger, etc.) In this country the laws of those states in which a judicial separation [111] may be obtained recognize quite generally the causes given in the Code. In one state the divorce from bed and board is prohibited and only the absolute divorce from the bond is admitted. In other states there is no positive legislation in regard to separation; and since there is no provision on the matter in the common law, a judicial separation cannot be obtained in those states. By the laws of still other states a separation will be granted only in favor of the wife.[112]

In one's approach to the problem of jurisdictional conflicts it must be pointed out in the beginning that questions of separation among the baptized (even if only one of the spouses be baptized) pertain exclusively to ecclesiastical judges.[113] Hence civil tribunals lack competence to hear and decide such cases, unless it be a matter involving the purely civil effects of marriage, and a case in which these civil effects are principally (and not merely incidentally or accessorily) in litigation.[114]

In the United States the civil authority has usurped the judicial power of the Church over the matrimonial causes of the baptized. In practice, therefore, to avoid grave harm the parties may have recourse to the civil courts for the purpose of obtaining a judicial

---

110 Adultery is an intrinsic cause in that it militates against the unity of marriage.

111 The term *judicial separation* is used in contradistinction to a merely *private separation.* A private separation accomplished by the mutual consent of the parties obtains no juridical effect.

112 For these variations in the civil provisions on separation, cf. Alford, *Ius Matrimoniale Comparatum,* n. 453.

113 Cf. canon 1960.

114 Cf. canon 1961.

separation that will be recognized in the eyes of the State; but to do this they must obtain permission from the local Ordinary.[115] In those states which either positively forbid, or make no provision for, separation from bed and board, it may be necessary for the innocent party to seek an absolute civil divorce; otherwise he or she will not have the full protection of the civil law in property rights and in regard to the custody of the children. And even in some of those states which do make provision for a separation *a mensa et thoro,* the full protection of law in regard to the rights of the innocent spouse can be secured only through the obtaining of an absolute civil divorce. But in these cases, likewise, baptized persons would have to obtain permission for this from the proper ecclesiastical authority; and, in seeking the divorce, the parties would have to do so with the sole intention of securing the civil effects and with the realization that this civil action would have no effect on the matrimonial bond itself.[116]

As to the civil provisions on separation so far as they affect the marriages of the unbaptized, these laws may be considered as proper and reasonable, provided that they do not admit abuse by granting separation for extrinsic causes that are inane or trivial, and provided that they do not attempt to touch the bond of such marriages. For the civil authority has no power to dissolve the bond of marriage even of its unbaptized subjects. Of this more will be said in the next section of this article.

B—CIVIL DIVORCE "A VINCULO"

In no other aspect is the civil legislation on marriage so diametrically opposed to the Catholic doctrine on marriage as it is in regard to divorce. In these laws by which the State arrogates to itself a supposed power to dissolve the bond of marriage (whether of Christians or of infidels), and to grant the consorts permission to contract another marriage, the civil authority is

[115] "Iis omnibus, qui matrimonio coniuncti sunt, praecipimus, ne inconsulta auctoritate ecclesiastica, tribunalia civilia adeant ad obtinendam separationem a thoro et mensa. Quod si quis attentaverit, sciat se gravem reatum incurrere et pro Epicopi indicio puniendum esse."—*Acta et Decreta Concilii Plenarii Baltimorensis Tertii A. D. MDCCCLXXXIV*, n. 126.

[116] Cf. Nau, *Marriage Laws of the Code,* n. 153, and n. 155, p. 200.

going beyond the sphere of its competence and is acting contrary to the divine law itself.[117] For marriage is intrinsically indissoluble by the primary precepts of the natural law and extrinsically indissoluble by the secondary precepts of the natural law.[118] This principle of indissolubility, founded in the law of nature, is sanctioned by the divine positive law—both by the rule of the original institution of marriage and by the law of the New Covenant.[119] Since marriage is by nature indissoluble, no merely human authority is competent to deal with the bond of marriage.[120]

But, on the other hand, since the primary end of marriage (the procreation and education of children) would not be radically defeated if it were lawful to dissolve marriage after this end was attained, neither the existence of marriage nor the good of society can be said to demand *absolute* indissolubility of the matrimonial bond.[121] Hence, a limited and restricted dissolubility, though con-

[117] Commenting on the obligation of the State to act according to the principles of legal justice and to observe in its laws the tenets of natural and divine positive law, Roelker says: " It is inconceivable that any law of the State can have any validity if it is contrary to the natural or divine law. . . . No legislator can enact a law contrary to the principles upon which his society and, therefore, his power are based. . . . Further, if the individuals are bound by another law of God, such as the doctrine of Christ in regard to matrimony, the State can not validly legislate against such a law as it would be acting entirely outside its competence."—" The State "—*The Ecclesiastical Review,* CVII (1942), 171.

[118] Intrinsic dissolubility is that by which the contract can be dissolved by the will of the contracting parties on their own private authority. Extrinsic dissolubility is that by which the matrimonial bond can be dissolved by a higher authority under certain circumstances and for certain restricted causes.—Cf. Merkelbach, *Summa Theologiae Moralis,* III, n. 816.

[119] Genesis, 2:24; Matthew, 19:3–8. Cf. De Smet, *Betrothment and Marriage,* nn. 324–325.

[120] Pius IX ("*Syllabus Errorum,*" prop. 67—Denzinger, n. 1767) condemned the proposition that marriage is not indissoluble by the law of nature and that in some cases absolute divorce can be decreed by the civil authority.

[121] The only type of marriage that is endowed with an absolute intrinsic and extrinsic indissolubility is a ratified and consummated Christian marriage. This quality of absolute indissolubility it derives from two elements taken together, viz., its sacramental character and the fact of consummation.—Cf. De Smet, *Betrothment and Marriage,* n. 367; also Cappello, *De Sacramentis,* III, n. 755, wherein other authors are cited on this point.

trary to the secondary precepts of the natural law, is possible under divine authority. For that reason it is true that among the baptized a ratified and unconsummated marriage, and among the unbaptized a legitimate and consummated marriage, can be dissolved under certain conditions determined by the divine law. This, however, can be done only by a power divinely conferred on the Church alone—and not at all by any power of the State.[122] As Alford observes: "Between this dissolution of the bond as provided by divine law and pernicious civil divorce no comparison can be made." [123]

The above principles in regard to the indissolubility of marriage and in regard to the exclusive authority of the Church over the bond, are nowhere set forth with more acumen or with more force than in the Encyclical of Pope Pius XI on Christian Marriage. He writes:

> And this inviolable stability, although not in the same perfect measure in every case, belongs to every true marriage, for the word of the Lord: "What God hath joined together let no man put asunder," must of necessity include all true marriages without exception, since it was spoken of the marriage of our first parents, the prototype of every future marriage . . . Wherefore, Our predecessor, Pius VI of happy memory, writing to the Bishop of Eger (Erlau), most wisely said: "Hence it is clear that marriage even in the state of nature and certainly long before it was raised to the dignity of a sacrament was divinely instituted in such a way that it should carry with it a perpetual and indissoluble bond which cannot therefore be dissolved by any civil law. Therefore although the sacramental element may be absent from a marriage as is the case among unbelievers, still in such a marriage, inasmuch as it is a true marriage there must remain and indeed there does remain that perpetual bond which by divine right is so bound up with matrimony from its first institution that it is not subject to any civil power . . ."

[122] Cf. canons 1118–1127; Wernz-Vidal, *Ius Matrimoniale*, nn. 619–638; De Smet, *Betrothment and Marriage*, nn. 328–355; Gasparri, *De Matrimonio*, nn. 1122–1170; Cappello, *De Sacramentis*, III, nn. 755–792.

[123] *Ius Matrimoniale Comparatum*, n. 441,

> And if this stability seems to be open to exception, however rare the exception may be, as in the case of certain natural marriages between unbelievers, or amongst Christians in the case of those marriages which though valid have not been consummated, that exception does not depend on the will of men nor on that of any merely human power, but on divine law, of which the only guardian and interpreter is the Church of Christ. However, not even this power can ever affect for any cause whatsoever a Christian marriage which is valid and has been consummated, for as it is plain that here the marriage contract has its full completion, so, by the will of God, there is also the greatest firmness and indissolubility which may not be destroyed by any human authority.[124]

C—CIVIL DECLARATION OF NULLITY

Between the civil and the canonical legislation regarding the declaration of nullity of a marriage there are some fundamental points of agreement and also some fundamental points of wide divergence. To go into a detailed discussion of these would be beyond the scope of this present study. But their importance for a thorough understanding of the matter is such that the reader would find it profitable to consult Alford's clear and concise comparison of these points.[125] Here it will be sufficient to consider the general principles involved and their application to this particular question.

As to the marriages of the unbaptized, the civil courts are competent to grant a declaration of nullity if the marriage was contracted in contravention of civil regulations—provided, of course, that such regulations are themselves not contrary to the natural or divine positive law. When by reason of some civil impediment a marriage between two infidels is regarded as absolutely void, a judicial declaration of the nullity is not strictly required according to the civil regulations of most of the states, but it nevertheless can be sought and obtained as a precautionary measure. On the other hand, in the event that such a marriage

---

[124] Ep. encycl. *Casti Connubii—AAS,* XXII (1930), 551–552; English translation from *Selected Papal Encyclicals* 1896 *to* 1931, I, 15–17.

[125] *Ius Matrimoniale Comparatum,* sectio 46.

is regarded as voidable by the civil law, then a judicial action is generally necessary. When in such actions the civil provisions attribute to the sentence a merely declaratory force so that the marriage is held to have been null *ab initio,* the State is not exceeding its competence. By the laws of some states, however, the judicial declaration in regard to a voidable marriage is considered as having a rescissory or annulling effect, so that the marriage is held to be invalid not from the beginning but only from the time of the declaration.[126] By this disposition of the civil law the judicial sentence in these cases is no longer a true declaration of nullity, even though it be designated by that term. Rather, it is a divorce from the matrimonial bond, and as such cannot be warranted.

In the question of declaration of nullity, as in other matters involving marriage legislation and jurisprudence, the chief source of practical conflict of competence between Church and State lies in the fact that the states in this country do not recognize the competence of ecclesiastical tribunals. The civil courts have usurped the judicial power of the Church to judge and pass sentence in the matrimonial causes of the baptized. For, as has already been seen, the State enjoys competence in these matters only with respect to the merely civil effects, and even then only if the civil effects are the principal object of the litigation.[127]

Yet the fact remains that the civil authority has arrogated to itself a judicial power over all marriages, whether of unbaptized persons or of baptized persons. In practice, to avoid open conflict with that authority and to prevent unjust and grave harm to themselves, it is often necessary for baptized consorts to seek (after obtaining proper ecclesiastical approval) a civil declaration of nullity of their marriage—or even a divorce if the nature

[126] This concept seems to derive from the fact that at civil law certain contracts whose fulfillment may be partially hampered are rescindible at the will of the parties. And although the marriage contract is not held to be voidable or rescindible by the parties themselves, yet the civil authority has assumed to itself the power to effect a rescission. But certainly by divine law marriage is irrescindible.

[127] Cf. *supra,* p. 95.

of the civil legislation should require such action.[128] But this, of course, must be done for the sole purpose of removing any civil obstacles to the freedom that may be conceded them only by the divine law and by canon law. Hence, a declaration of nullity that will have for their marriage the true juridical effect connoted in the term must still be obtained from the competent ecclesiastical tribunal, or from the proper ecclesiastical authority if it be a case comprehended by the norms of canon 1990.

Article 5

Compliance of Catholics with Civil Regulations

Certain it is that the competence of the Church is not limited to the marriages of Catholics but extends to the marriages of all Christians. For practical reasons, however, the present article is restricted to a discussion of Catholic compliance with civil regulations on marriage. But what is said of such compliance on the part of Catholics will, other things being equal and due allowance being made for particular circumstances, apply likewise to the observance of the same regulations on the part of baptized non-Catholics.

It has been shown that the State acts within its proper sphere of authority when it enacts certain prescriptions that pertain to the purely civil effects of marriage.[129] Conformity of Catholics with such laws is rightly to be expected: with these matters the present discussion is not concerned. But within the present chapter it has already been pointed out that State marriage laws are legislated and applied in such a way as to present many points of conflict with the jurisdiction of the Church. The problem of Catholic compliance with these laws is of extreme practical importance. It will be of interest, then, to make some inquiry into that compliance, to determine whether it may be admitted, and, if so, to

---

[128] Cf. Wernz-Vidal, *Ius Matrimoniale,* n. 711, note 13; Payen, *De Matrimonio,* II, n. 2512; Alford, *Ius Matrimoniale Comparatum,* n. 432; Kay, *Competence in Matrimonial Procedure* (The Catholic University of America Canon Law Studies, n. 53, Washington, D. C.: The Catholic University of America, 1929), 42–45.

[129] Cf. *supra,* p. 58.

what extent and on what grounds. The factors fundamental to the discussion are both theological and juridical. The first must necessarily be given some consideration, but the character of the present study demands that greater attention be paid to the second.

It has, in fact, previously been noted that when civil matrimonial regulations are invalid for Catholics—invalid for them because the State has legislated outside its own sphere of competence—the Church permits Catholics to observe such laws as long as they are proper, that is, as long as they are not contrary to the natural or the divine positive law or detrimental to the Church.[130] It has been seen, too, that compliance with these regulations is justified theologically on the basis of the precept of charity; that there is a certain obligation to observe these laws—an obligation that arises not from the laws themselves but from the precept of charity.[131]

Considering the question, then, from a theological viewpoint, one may state that Catholics may comply with civil regulations that infringe upon the competence of the Church, provided that these regulations do not exact or presuppose contraventions of the law of God and are not positively harmful to the Church. Fundamentally, the attitude of the Church towards this compliance is founded in her maternal solicitude for the temporal as well as the spiritual welfare of souls. Pope Leo XIII takes cognizance of this disposition of the Church when he says: "It is of the greatest consequence to husband and wife that all these things [scil., concerning the origin, nature, ends, properties, and regulation of marriage] should be well known and understood by them, in order *that they may conform to the laws of the State, if there be no objection on the part of the Church;* for the Church wishes the effects of marriage to be guarded in all possible ways, and that no harm may come to the children." [132]

Such, then, is the theological approach to the problem. But

---

[130] Cf. *supra*, p. 57.

[131] Cf. *supra*, pp. 59–60.

[132] Ep. encycl. *Arcanum Divinae,* 10 feb. 1880, §25—*Fontes,* n. 580; *The Pope and the People,* 42. (Italics supplied by the writer.)

before considering in detail the juridical aspect one may well observe that herein lies another striking illustration of the intimate and harmonious interrelation of theological and juridical principles. The central link in this case is charity. Commenting on charity as " an ethical and legal fundamental ideal which fills the Law of the Church with the fullness of humanity," Plöchl quite appositely remarks: " It is true, the Law of the Church is strict in its unchangeable Divine and Natural principles. But it is also the law of charity. It is ruled by charity . . . [charity] is the sublime norm, guiding the spirit of the Code in its every phase. It is the basic principle of distributive justice, the supreme criterion of every aspect of the Law of the Church." [133] It is obvious from this that the fundamental ideal of charity is basic to both the theological and the juridical elements involved in the problem under consideration. Prescinding for the time from that factor, one has now to inquire into the essentially juridical phase of the question, and to seek to determine the juridical grounds which support and justify Catholic compliance with civil regulations on marriage.

Approaching the matter first from the standpoint of the rights of Church and State, one should note that in this country the conflict of competence arises proximately from a usurpation of power. The State does not deny to the Church the *right* to legislate for Christian marriages, but it does deny the *exclusiveness* of that right. The State has assumed to itself a power that properly and rightly belongs to the Church. But in exercising this usurped power the secular authority seldom if ever acts from motives of positive hostility towards the Church. This fact in itself makes the problem of conformity to civil prescriptions less difficult, for, although there are certain fundamental contrarieties between the two systems of law, still there are many elements of concord which provide a basis for a composition of the difficulties. Hence the Church is able to accommodate herself to practically all civil regulations without great inconvenience; and this she is willing to do as long as there is not required any abandonment of

[133] "Fundamental Principles of the Philosophy of Canon Law."—*The Jurist* (Washington, D. C., 1941—), IV (1944), 97-98.

principle. As Pope Leo XIII says: ". . . the Catholic Church, though powerless in any way to abandon the duties of her office or the defence of her authority, still very greatly inclines to kindness and indulgence whenever they are consistent with the safety of her rights and the sanctity of her duties. Wherefore she makes no decrees in relation to marriage without having regard to the state of the body politic and condition of the general public; and has besides more than once mitigated, as far as possible, the enactments of her own laws, when there were just and weighty reasons." [134]

An example in point may be found in the way in which the Church meets the requirement for civil authorization to assist at marriages which is enacted in the laws of some states. The Church, fully aware that her own authorization is sufficient for the validity of assistance at marriage on the part of her priests, yet has them secure the necessary civil authorization. By thus meeting this secular prescription the Church can be assured that, other things being equal, the civil effects will be conceded by the State to a marriage solemnized according to the canonical form.

It seems, moreover, that a further juridical basis for the observance by Catholics of secular marriage laws can be established from the practice of the ecclesiastical courts in matrimonial causes. Among the documents usually required of parties by the ecclesiastical tribunals are the documents of civil divorce. Wanenmacher makes the following comments on this practice: "In matters where the civil courts are not competent, such as when they declare marriage between Christians invalid, the dispositive part of such a decision has no value. Yet in nearly every case of nullity, Pauline privilege, or dispensation from ratified marriage, tried in diocesan court, it is necessary to present the papers of civil divorce. This is the common practice and is prescribed in some dioceses." [135] This is done not only for the purpose of securing possibly useful information, but also with the aim to avoid con-

---

[134] Ep. encycl. *Arcanum Divinae,* 10 feb. 1880, §21—*Fontes,* n. 580; *The Pope and the People,* 40.

[135] *Canonical Evidence in Marriage Cases* (Philadelphia: Dolphin Press, 1935), n. 345.

flict with the civil law which does not acknowledge the competence of the ecclesiastical tribunal, and to protect the parties from a consequent civil charge of bigamy.[136] In such matters, again, there is no departure from principle, for it is a question not of requiring a divorce *as a divorce,* but rather of complying with a secular legal formality in order to secure civil recognition for an act of ecclesiastical jurisdiction that is complete in itself.

Certainly it would be to the advantage of both Church and State in this country if through some formal agreement a definite settlement of the various points of conflict could be effected. But the absence of such an express agreement does not necessarily militate against the existence of an amicable functioning of these two authorities. The practical manner in which the difficulties and problems have been met by the Church in this country, together with the at least benevolent (even if patronizing) disposition of the State towards the Church, have resulted in the establishment of an implied *modus vivendi.* Such an arrangement, because not founded on any mutual understanding as to principles, has the obvious disadvantage of providing a somewhat tenuous juridical basis for settling any particular matter of conflict; but, on the other hand, it has averted, in an acceptable manner, the practical burgeoning of many potential theoretical conflicts.

From this implicit *modus vivendi* there has developed in this country an almost universal practice to observe the civil regulations on marriage within certain limits, i.e., within limits consonant with the safety of the rights of the Church and consistent with the sanctity of her duties. This compliance is not only manifested by priests and bishops; it is also encouraged and at times even required of the faithful by them. It seems, moreover, that this mode of acting, especially since it has developed in such a way as to secure the unhampered functioning of ecclesiastical jurisdiction and at the same time to procure the protection in civil law of the rights of the spouses, may be said to have at least the tacit approval of the Holy See.

---

136 Doheny, *Canonical Procedure in Matrimonial Cases* (Milwaukee: Bruce, 1938), 286–287; cf. also Hannan, "Civil Divorce Requisite for Ecclesiastical Adjudication?"—*The Jurist,* IV (1944), 160–161.

If the matter be regarded from the standpoint of the individual and his rights, it appears that there are certain other juridical factors that justify his compliance with the civil regulations in question. The right to marry, as has often been noted in the course of this study, is one of the innate rights that man has from the natural law. Further determined by the divine positive law, this right to marry receives a formal declaration in the Code of Canon Law.[137] Around this right is built up a system of rules embodying not only the principles of natural and divine positive law, but also the further determinations of ecclesiastical law. Through the norms of the Church law the principles of the divine law are determined to more definite purposes—but always with a view to the most effective preservation and application of these principles. It is recognized that in particular cases there may sometimes arise a difficulty in harmonizing the fulfillment of the positive specifications with the attainment of the fundamental rights envisaged in the principles themselves.

It is at this point that the principle of equity enters to effect the operation of the natural law over and beyond the human positive law. And where even this natural equity fails to solve the disparity between justice and a strict application of the law, there is a last resort in the principle of *epicheia,* or personal equity. In the right application of these principles of justice and equity there exists a solid juridical basis for the observance by Catholics (within the limits already explained) of the civil regulations on marriage. The recognition and development of these principles flow directly from that basic charity in the law of the Church which, though leaving intact the strictness of that law, yet removes from it any semblance of a cold and unsympathetic formalism. More remotely, this operation of the law of the Church flows from the supernatural aim of the Church—which is the sanctification and salvation of souls.

What has been said thus far regarding compliance with civil laws applies principally to the positive prescriptions of these laws. A final observation must be made concerning the civil laws which in their prohibitory provisions trespass upon the competence of

[137] Canon 1035.

the Church. For a Catholic, under ordinary circumstances, these prohibitions will work no great hardship. The Church generally encourages Catholics to observe them not only to avoid conflict with the State but also to promote their own good and the public welfare. It has already been noted that though the Church forbids neither interracial marriage nor the marriage of persons afflicted with a communicable social disease, still in general she does discourage such unions.[138]

The Church, unlike the State, realizes that at times and in particular cases there may be just reasons or excusing causes in conscience that will justify such marriages. But since the State does not recognize the existence of excusing causes, the law prohibiting these marriages is applied strictly in all cases, and violators are subject to severe civil penalties. Since such a law is invalid for a Catholic (and even unjust, in the hypothesis that there are excusing causes), he would be justified in going into another state where the prohibition does not exist, in order there to contract marriage before a priest and two witnesses according to the substantial canonical form.

When for one reason or another this solution of the problem would be impracticable (as might be the case if the parties were very poor), Catholics wishing to contract marriage under the circumstances outlined could do so before two witnesses alone, according to the norm of canon 1098.[139] The use of this latter form will, of course, effect a valid and licit marriage in the eyes of the Church, but the marriage will remain without any recognition before the secular law.

---

[138] Cf. *supra*, pp. 85 and 66–67.

[139] Cf. *Pontificia Commissio Interpretationis,* 25 iul. 1931—*AAS,* XXIII (1931), 388. In the reply of the Commission it is stated that the physical absence of the pastor or Ordinary, as comprehended by canon 1098, includes also the case in which either of them, though materially present, cannot by reason of grave inconvenience assist at the marriage. Gasparri (*De Matrimonio,* n. 1017), commenting on this response of the Code Commission, states that the grave inconvenience which the Commission had in mind is that which may arise from a civil law which forbids marriage under grave penalties.

CONCLUSIONS

1. The Decretals do not, so far as the writer has been able to determine, contain any express assertion of the right of the Church and the extent of her jurisdiction over marriage. But the very existence and scope of a comprehensive matrimonial legislation in the law of the Church at that time presents a forcible argument in favor of the fact and the extent of her competence over marriage. This statement is supported by the evidence found in the decretal material treating of matters intimately connected with marriage, as, e.g., dowry rights and inheritance rights. Whenever jurisdictional disputes or problems arose in such cases, they were settled according to the basic principle that matters of a spiritual and sacred character are under the jurisdiction of the Church and those of a temporal and secular nature are under the jurisdiction of the State.

2. Canonists are in general agreement that the Church is the competent authority for the marriages of the baptized among themselves, and the State for the marriages of the unbaptized among themselves. There is, however, a diversity of opinion among canonists regarding the competent authority over marriages between the baptized and the unbaptized. Some hold that the civil law binds for the unbaptized and canon law for the baptized, and that the prescriptions of each must be met by the respective subjects of these laws. Others maintain that the civil law does not enter into consideration, and that such marriages are governed by canon law alone. Both opinions must be regarded as probable, but the intrinsic arguments in favor of the second are such as to make it the more probable opinion. This second opinion, moreover, is certainly in harmony with the fundamental juridical principle that in the event of a conflict of competence over a *res mixta* the rights of the Church, inasmuch as they pertain to a higher order, should prevail.

3. The remote source of the chief points in the conflict of jurisdiction is to be found in the lack of co-operation on the part

of the State towards the achievement and preservation of an harmonious functioning of Church and State in the attainment of their respective aims and purposes. More proximately, these conflicts arise from a usurpation of authority by the State—a usurpation that is crystallized in the legislation and application of civil marriage laws for all subjects of the State, irrespective of the rights of the Church over the baptized.

4. It is admitted that the State is competent to legislate for the purely civil effects of Christian marriage. But this competence must be understood strictly. Hence, whenever the scope of secular legislation extends beyond the merely civil effects and touches either upon the substance itself or upon the inseparable effects of the marital bond, the obligation arising from the civil law itself to observe these regulations is no longer binding upon Christians. However, to avoid harm to themselves or to their children, Christians may at times be bound by a precept of charity to comply with these regulations, provided that such regulations are not contrary to the natural or divine positive law and are not harmful to the rights of the Church.

5. With regard to social disease legislation of the State the following points are to be noted in the matter of Christian marriage:

(a) The civil authority may not in such wise prescribe a medical examination for baptized persons about to be married that, if this condition is not fulfilled, marriage either is forbidden to them, or, if contracted, will be deprived of its validity or civil effects. By so doing the State would be establishing an impediment either directly or indirectly, and this the State is entirely incompetent to do for Christian marriages.

(b) Granted that the State would act within its proper sphere of competence if it segregated the diseased persons until a cure could be effected, it does not follow that the State may on the basis of that authority restrain them from marrying without such segregation. To forbid marriage even temporarily to baptized persons afflicted with some venereal infection, the State would have to act in harmony and in co-operation with the competent authority for the baptized, i.e., the Church.

(c) The assignment to the State of such power over Christian marriage cannot be justified on the grounds of the right of the State to enforce the natural law. It is the teaching of the majority of theologians that, given the requisite justifying causes, the natural law does not forbid the marriage of a person afflicted with a communicable social disease. Whether in a given case it would or would not be against the natural law for a baptized person so infected to marry, it would be the right and duty of the Church, and not of the State, to determine.

6. Insofar as civil impediments in general are concerned, they cannot affect the intrinsic validity or lawfulness of a Christian marriage contracted in accordance with the norms of the law of the Church, which alone is competent to establish impediments, over and above those of the divine law, for such marriages.

7. Baptized non-Catholics are not bound by civil requirements as to the form of marriage, for the Church is solely competent to determine the form, beyond that required by the natural law, for Christian marriage. But according to canon 1099, §2, certain baptized persons are exempted from the observance of the canonical form. Hence, these persons are bound only by the form required by the natural law, viz., mutual consent externally and reciprocally manifested through words or signs by persons capable of contracting marriage.

8. Compliance of Catholics with civil regulations on marriage in this country may be permitted, provided that this compliance be within established limits consonant with the right of the Church and consistent with the sanctity of her doctrine on marriage. Such compliance is justified theologically on the basis of the precept of charity, and juridically on the basis of a right application of the principles of justice and equity. This juridical basis is further augmented by the general practice of observing secular marriage laws within the limits mentioned above—a practice that seems to be founded in an implicit *modus vivendi* which has developed between the State and the Church in this country.

BIBLIOGRAPHY

SOURCES

Acta Apostolicae Sedis, Commentarium Officiale, Romae, 1909——

Acta et Decreta Concilii Plenarii Baltimorensis Tertii, A.D. MDCCCLXXXIV, Baltimorae, 1886.

Acta Sanctae Sedis, 41 vols., Romae, 1865–1908.

Canones et Decreta Sacrosanctae Oecumenici Concilii Tridentini, Taurini, 1913.

Codex Iuris Canonici Pii X Pontificis Maximi iussu digestus, Benedicti Papae XV auctoritate promulgatus, Romae: Typis Polyglottis Vaticanis, 1917.

Codicis Iuris Canonici Fontes cura Eñi. Card. Gasparri editi, 9 vols., Romae (postea, Civitate Vaticana): Typis Polyglottis Vaticanis, 1923–1939. (Vols. VII-IX *ed. cura et studio Eñi. Iustiniani Card. Serédi.*)

Collectanea S. Congregationis de Propaganda Fide, 2 vols., Romae: Typographia Polyglotta S. C. de Propaganda Fide, 1907.

Corpus Iuris Canonici, editio Lipsiensis secunda post Aemilii Ludovici Richteri curas instruxit Aemilius Friedberg, 1879–1881. Editio anastatice repetita, Lipsiae: Tauchnitz, 1928.

Corpus Iuris Civilis, 3 vols., Berolini, 1928–1929. *Institutiones,* quas recognovit P. Krueger; *Digesta,* quas recognovit T. Mommsen et retractavit P. Krueger; *Codex Iustinianus,* quem recognovit et retractavit P. Krueger; *Novellae,* quas recognovit R. Schoell, et absolvit G. Kroll.

Decretales D. Gregorii Papae IX, una cum glossis restitutae, 2 vols., Romae, 1582.

Decretum Gratiani emendatum et notationibus illustratum una cum glossis, 2 vols., Romae, 1582.

Enchiridion Symbolorum Definitionum et Declarationum de Rebus Fidei et Morum, edd. H. Denzinger, C. Bannwart, J. Umberg, 21.–23. ed., Friburgi Brisgoviae: Herder & Co., 1937.

Jaffé, Philippus, *Regesta Pontificum Romanorum ab condita Ecclesia ad annum post Christum natum* MCXCVIII, 2. ed. (Kaltenbrunner, Ewald, Loewenfeld), 2 vols. in 1, Lipsiae, 1885–1888.

Liber Sextus Decretalium D. Bonifacii Papae VIII, Romae, 1582.

Papal Encyclicals and Letters 1896 *to* 1931, *Selected, Vol. I,* London: Catholic Truth Society, 1939.

Pope and the People, The (*Select Letters and Addresses on Social Questions*), London: Catholic Truth Society, 1937.

POTTHAST, A., *Regesta Pontificum,* 2 vols., Berolini, 1874–1875.

Quinque Compilationes Antiquae, ed. Aemilius Friedberg, Lipsiae, 1882.

SCHROEDER, H. J., *Canons and Decrees of the Council of Trent: Original Text with English Translation,* St. Louis: B. Herder Book Co., 1941.

REFERENCE WORKS

AERTNYS, J.-Damen, C. A., *Theologia Moralis secundum doctrinam S. Alfonsi de Liguori,* 12. ed., 2 vols., Taurinorum Augustae: Marietti, 1932.

ALFORD, CULVER BERNARDUS, *Ius Matrimoniale Comparatum,* Romae: Anonima Libraria Cattolica Italiana, 1938.

AYRINHAC, H. A.-LYDON, P. J., *Marriage Legislation in the New Code of Canon Law,* new revised ed., New York: Benziger Bros., 1938.

BOUSCAREN, T. LINCOLN, *The Canon Law Digest,* 2 vols., Milwaukee: The Bruce Publishing Company, 1934–1943.

CAPPELLO, FELIX M., *Institutiones Iuris Publici Ecclesiastici,* 2 vols., Taurinorum Augustae, 1907–1908.

———, *Tractatus Canonico-Moralis de Sacramentis,* Vol. III, *De Matrimonio,* ed. quarta emendata et aucta, Romae: Marietti, 1939.

CATHREIN, VICTOR, *Philosophia Moralis, Cursus Philosophicus, pars VI,* ed. decima quinta, Friburgi Brisgoviae: Herder & Co., 1929.

CAVAGNIS, FELIX, *Institutiones Iuris Publici Ecclesiastici,* 4. ed., 3 vols., Romae, 1906.

CHELODI, IOANNES, *Ius Matrimoniale,* ed. quarta, recognita et aucta a V. Dalpiaz, Tridenti: Libreria Moderna Editrice A. Ardesi, 1937.

CORONATA, MATTHAEUS CONTE A, *Ius Publicum Ecclesiasticum,* 2. ed., Taurini: Marietti, 1934.

DAVIS, HENRY, *Moral and Pastoral Theology,* 2 ed., 4 vols., New York: Sheed & Ward, 1936.

DEBECKER, IULIUS, *De Matrimonio Praelectiones Canonicae,* ed. nova, Louvain: Fr. Ceutrick, 1931.

DE SMET, AL., *Tractatus Theologico-Canonicus De Sponsalibus et Matrimonio,* ed. quarta inde a Codice altera, Brugis: Car. Beyaert, Editor Pontificius, 1927.

———, *Betrothment and Marriage,* 2. ed., trans. from the 3rd Latin edition of 1920 by W. Dobell, 2 vols., Brugis: Charles Beyaert, 1923.

DILLON, ROBERT E., *Common Law Marriage,* The Catholic University of America Canon Law Studies, n. 153, Washington, D. C.: The Catholic University of America Press, 1942.

DOHENY, WILLIAM J., *Canonical Procedure in Matrimonial Cases,* Milwaukee: The Bruce Publishing Company, 1938.

ESMEIN, A., *Le Mariage en Droit Canonique,* 2. ed., 2 vols. (Vol. I rev. by R. Génestal, 1929, Vol. II rev. by R. Génestal & J. Dauvillier, 1935), Paris: Librairie de Recueil Sirey, 1929–1935.

FARRELL, WALTER, *A Companion to the Summa*, 4 vols., New York: Sheed & Ward, 1939–1942, Vol. IV, *The Way of Life*, 1942.

GASPARRI, PETRUS CARD., *Tractatus Canonicus de Matrimonio*, ed. nova ad mentem Codicis I. C., 2 vols. in 1, Romae: Typis Polyglottis Vaticanis, 1932.

GRANDCLAUDE, E., *Ius Canonicum*, 3 vols., Parisiis, 1882–1883.

HOSTIENSIS, (Henricus de Segusio), *Henrici Cardinalis Hostiensis Summa Aurea*, Lugduni, 1568.

———, *In Quinque Decretalium Libros Commentaria*, Venetiis, 1581.

JOYCE, G. H., *Christian Marriage: An Historical and Doctrinal Study*, London: Sheed & Ward, 1933.

KAY, THOMAS H., *Competence in Matrimonial Procedure*, The Catholic University of America Canon Law Studies, n. 53, Washington, D. C.: The Catholic University of America, 1929.

LA FARGE, JOHN, *The Race Question and the Negro*, New York: Longmans, Green & Co., 1943.

MERKELBACH, BENEDICTUS HENRICUS, *Summa Theologiae Moralis*, editio altera aucta et emendata, 3 vols., Parisiis: Desclée de Brouwer et Soc., 1935–36.

NAU, LOUIS J., *Manual on the Marriage Laws of the Code of Canon Law*, 2. ed., New York and Cincinnati: Frederick Pustet Co., Inc., 1934.

OTTAVIANI, ALAPHRIDUS, *Institutiones Iuris Publici Ecclesiastici*, 2. ed., 2 vols., Civitate Vaticana: Typis Polyglottis Vaticanis, 1935–1936.

PANORMITANUS (Nicholas de Tudeschis), *Nicolai Tudeschii Catiensis Siculi Panormitani Archiepiscopi vulgo Abbatis Panormitani Omnia quae extant Commentaria in Decretalium Libros*, 10 tomes, Venetiis, 1588.

PAYEN, G., *De Matrimonio in Missionibus et Potissimum in Sinis Tractatus Practicus et Casus*, 2. ed., 3 vols., Zi-ka-wei: In typographia T'ou-sè-wè, 1935–1936.

PETROVITS, JOSEPH J. C., *The New Church Law on Matrimony*, 2. ed., Philadelphia: John Joseph McVey, 1926.

PFATSCHBACHER, HERMAN, *Eugenische Ehehindernisse*, eine kirchenrechtliche Studie, Theologische Studien der Österreichischen Leo-Gesellschaft, herausgegeben von Dr. Leopold Krebs und Dr. Josef Lehner, n. 34, Wien: Verlag Mayer und Comp., 1933.

PIRHING, ERNRICUS, *Ius Canonicum Nova Methodo Explicatum*, 5 vols., Dilingae, 1674–1678.

ROBINSON, WILLIAM C., *Elementary Law*, rev. ed., Boston, 1910.

SABETTI, A.-BARRETT, T., *Compendium Theologiae Moralis*, 8. ed. post Codicem, Neo Eboraci: Frederick Pustet Co., Inc., 1939.

SANCHEZ, THOMAS, *Disputationum de Sancto Matrimonii Sacramento Tomi Tres*, Antverpiae, 1652.

SCHMALZGRUEBER, FRANCISCUS, *Ius Ecclesiaticum Universum,* 5 vols. in 12, Romae, 1843–1845.

SMITH, W. D., *Handbook of Elementary Law,* 2. ed. by A. H. McGray, St. Paul: West Publishing Co., 1939.

TANQUEREY, AD., *De Poenitentia et Matrimonio, Pars Dogmatica,* 4. ed., Parisiis: Desclée et Socii, 1930.

——, *Synopsis Theologiae Dogmaticae Fundamentalis,* 23. ed., Parisiis: Desclée et Socii, 1930.

TARQUINI, CAMILLUS, *Institutiones Iuris Ecclesiastici Publici,* 4. ed., Romae, 1865.

THOMAS AQUINAS, ST., *Summa Theologica,* 5 vols., Taurini: Marietti, 1932.

——, *Summa Contra Gentiles,* Taurini: Marietti, 1937.

VERMEERSCH, A., *What is Marriage?* transl. by T. L. Bouscaren, New York: The America Press, 1932.

VERMEERSCH, A.-CREUSEN, J., *Epitome Iuris Canonici,* 3 vols., Vol. I, 6. ed., 1937; Vols. II-III, 5. ed., 1936, Mechliniae-Romae: H. Dessain.

Vlaming, Th.M., *Praelectiones Iuris Matrimonialis,* 3. ed. 2 vols., Bussum in Hollandia, 1919–1921.

VROMANT, G. *Ius Missionariorum de Matrimonio,* ed. altera emendata, Parisiis: Desclée, 1938.

WANENMACHER, FRANCIS, *Canonical Evidence in Marriage Cases,* Philadelphia: Dolphin Press, 1935.

WERNZ, FRANCISCUS X., *Ius Decretalium,* Vol. I, *Introductio in Ius Decretalium,* altera editio emendata et aucta, Romae, 1905.

——, *Ius Decretalium,* Vol. IV, *Ius Matrimoniale Ecclesiae Catholicae,* Romae, 1904.

WERNZ-VIDAL, *Ius Canonicum,* 7 vols. in 8, Vol. V, *Ius Matrimoniale,* Romae: apud Aedes Universitatis Gregorianae, 1925.

ZOLLMANN, CARL, *American Church Law,* St. Paul: West Publishing Co., 1933.

ARTICLES

CONNELL, FRANCIS J., "May the State Forbid Marriage because of Social Disease?"—*The Ecclesiastical Review,* XCIX (1938), 507–518.

DONNELLY, FRANCIS B., AND CONNELL, FRANCIS J., "Compulsory Blood Tests before Marriage,"—*The Ecclesiastical Review,* CI (1939), 9–30.

GILLIGAN, FRANCIS J., "The Color Line Considered Morally,"—*The Ecclesiastical Review,* LXXXI (1929), 482–487.

GRANDCLAUDE, E., "Compétence de l'État Touchant le Mariage des Infideles," —*Le Canoniste Contemporain,* X (1887), 241–257.

HANNAN, JEROME D., "Civil Divorce Requisite for Ecclesiastical Adjudication?"—*The Jurist,* IV (1944), 160–161.

MOORE, THOMAS V., AND CONNELL, FRANCIS J., "Marriage and Venereal Infection,"—*The Ecclesiastical Review,* C (1939), 323–337.

OESTERLE, G., "De iure in missionibus matrimoniali,"—*Commentarium pro Religiosis et Missionariis,* XVII (1936), 257-270.

ONCLIN, W., "De regimine Matrimonii Fidelem inter et Infidelem,"—*Ephemerides Theologicae Lovanienses,* X (1933), 47-62.

PLÖCHL, WILLIBALD, "The Fundamental Principles of the Philosophy of Canon Law," —*The Jurist,* IV (1944), 70-100.

ROELKER, EDWARD G., "The State,"—*The Ecclesiastical Review,* CVII (1942), 161-176.

PERIODICALS

Canoniste Contemporain, Le, Paris, 1878-1924 (later, *Le Canoniste,* Paris, 1924-1926).

Commentarium pro Religiosis et Missionariis (originally, before 1935, *Commentarium pro Religiosis*), Romae, 1920——.

Ecclesiastical Review, The (originally and again from January, 1944, *The American Ecclesiastical Review*), Philadelphia (after 1943, Washington, D. C.), 1889——.

Ephemerides Theologicae Lovanienses, Lovanii, 1924——.

Jurist, The, Washington, D. C., 1941——.

ABBREVIATIONS

AAS—Acta Apostolicae Sedis
ASS—Acta Sanctae Sedis
C.—*Codex Iustinianus*
Collectanea—Collectanea Sacrae Congregationis de Propaganda Fide
Fontes—Codicis Iuris Canonici Fontes
N.—*Novellae Iustinianae*
R.J.—*Regula Iuris*

BIOGRAPHICAL NOTE

James William Goldsmith was born March 15, 1912, in Atlanta, Georgia. He received his elementary and high school education in the public schools of that city. In 1930 he entered the School of Commerce of the Georgia School of Technology, in Atlanta, and was graduated in 1934 with the degree of Bachelor of Commercial Science. In the same year he returned to that institution to begin a course of graduate study; after one year of graduate work he left to enter Saint Mary's Seminary in Baltimore to begin his studies for the priesthood. He completed his course of philosophy at Saint Mary's in 1937, and was assigned to the Theological College of the Catholic University of America. From the latter institution he received the degree of the Licentiate in Sacred Theology in June 1941, and was ordained to the priesthood on June 7, 1941. In September of that same year he returned to the Catholic University to enroll in the School of Canon Law, where he received the degree of the Baccalaureate in Canon Law in May 1942, and the degree of the Licentiate in Canon Law in May 1943.

INDEX

CANON LAW STUDIES*

1. FRERIKS, REV. CELESTINE A., C.PP.S., J.C.D., Religious Congregations in Their External Relations, 121 pp., 1916.
2. GALLIHER, REV. DANIEL M., O.P., J.C.D., Canonical Elections, 117 pp., 1917.
3. BORKOWSKI, REV. AURELIUS L., O.F.M., J.C.D., De Confraternitatibus Ecclesiasticis, 136 pp., 1918.
4. CASTILLO, REV. CAYO, J.C.D., Disertacion Historico-Canonica sobre la Potestad del Cabildo en Sede Vacante o Impedida del Vicario Capitular, 99 pp., 1919 (1918).
5. KUBELBECK, REV. WILLIAM J., S.T.B., J.C.D., The Sacred Penitentiaria and Its Relation to Faculties of Ordinaries and Priests, 129 pp., 1918.
6. PETROVITS, REV. JOSEPH, J. C., S.T.D., J.C.D., The New Church Law on Matrimony, X-461 pp., 1919.
7. HICKEY, REV. JOHN J., S.T.B., J.C.D., Irregularities and Simple Impediments in the New Code of Canon Law, 100 pp., 1920.
8. KLEKOTKA, REV. PETER J., S.T.B., J.C.D., Diocesan Consultors, 179 pp., 1920.
9. WANENMACHER, REV. FRANCIS, J.C.D., The Evidence in Ecclesiastical Procedure Affecting the Marriage Bond, 1920 (Printed 1935).
10. GOLDEN, REV. HENRY FRANCIS, J.C.D., Parochial Benefices in the New Code, IV-119 pp., 1921 (Printed 1925).
11. KOUDELKA, REV. CHARLES J., J.C.D., Pastors, Their Rights and Duties According to the New Code of Canon Law, 211 pp., 1921.
12. MELO, REV. ANTONIUS, O.F.M., J.C.D., De Exemptione Regularium, X-188 pp., 1921.
13. SCHAAF, REV. VALENTINE THEODORE, O.F.M., S.T.B., J.C.D., The Cloister, X-180 pp., 1921.
14. BURKE, REV. THOMAS JOSEPH, S.T.D., J.C.D., Competence in Ecclesiastical Tribunals, IV-117 pp., 1922.
15. LEECH, REV. GEORGE LEO, J.C.D., A Comparative Study of the Constitution "Apostolicae Sedis" and the "Codex Juris Canonici," 179 pp., 1922.
16. MOTRY, REV. HUBERT LOUIS, S.T.D., J.C.D., Diocesan Faculties According to the Code of Canon Law, II-167 pp., 1922.
17. MURPHY, REV. GEORGE LAWRENCE, J.C.D., Delinquencies and Penalties in the Administration and the Reception of the Sacraments, IV-121 pp., 1923.

* Below n. 100 only the following numbers are still available: Nn. 3, 4, 9, 25, 34, 57 and 75. Beginning with n. 100 only the following are unavailable: Nn. 100-111 inclusive, and n. 113.

18. O'Reilly, Rev. John Anthony, S.T.B., J.C.D., Ecclesiastical Sepulture in the New Code of Canon Law, II-129 pp., 1923.
19. Michalicka, Rev. Wenceslas Cyril, O.S.B., J.C.D., Judicial Procedure in Dismissal of Clerical Exempt Religious, 107 pp., 1923.
20. Dargin, Rev. Edward Vincent, S.T.B., J.C.D., Reserved Cases According to the Code of Canon Law, IV-103 pp., 1924.
21. Godfrey, Rev. John A., S.T.B., J.C.D., The Right of Patronage According to the Code of Canon Law, 153 pp., 1924.
22. Hagedorn, Rev. Francis Edward, J.C.D., General Legislation on Indulgences, II-154 pp., 1924.
23. King, Rev. James Ignatius, J.C.D., The Administration of the Sacraments to Dying Non-Catholics, V-141 pp., 1924.
24. Winslow, Rev. Francis Joseph, O.F.M., J.C.D., Vicars and Prefects Apostolic, IV-149 pp., 1924.
25. Correa, Rev. Jose Servelion, S.T.L., J.C.D., La Potestad Legislativa de la Iglesia Catolica, IV-127 pp., 1925.
26. Dugan, Rev. Henry Francis, A.M., J.C.D., The Judiciary Department of the Diocesan Curia, 87 pp., 1925.
27. Keller, Rev. Charles Frederick, S.T.B., J.C.D., Mass Stipends, 167 pp., 1925.
28. Paschang, Rev. John Linus, J.C.D., The Sacramentals According to the Code of Canon Law, 129 pp., 1925.
29. Piontek, Rev. Cyrillus, O.F.M., S.T.B., J.C.D., De Indulto Exclaustrationis necnon Saecularizationis, XIII-289 pp., 1925.
30. Kearney, Rev. Richard Joseph, S.T.B., J.C.D., Sponsors at Baptism According to the Code of Canon Law, IV-127 pp., 1925.
31. Bartlett, Rev. Chester Joseph, A.M., LL.B., J.C.D., The Tenure of Parochial Property in the United States of America, V-108 pp., 1926.
32. Kilker, Rev. Adrian Jerome, J.C.D., Extreme Unction, V-425 pp., 1926.
33. McCormick, Rev. Robert Emmett, J.C.D., Confessors of Religious, VIII-266 pp., 1926.
34. Miller, Rev. Newton Thomas, J.C.D., Founded Masses According to the Code of Canon Law, VII-93 pp., 1926.
35. Roelker, Rev. Edward G., S.T.D., J.C.D., Principles of Privilege According to the Code of Canon Law, XI-166 pp., 1926.
36. Bakalarczyk, Rev. Richardus, M.I.C., J.U.D., De Novitiatu, VIII-208 pp., 1927.
37. Pizzuti, Rev. Lawrence, O.F.M., J.U.L., De Parochis Religiosis, 1927. (Not Printed.)
38. Bliley, Rev. Nicholas Martin, O.S.B., J.C.D., Altars According to the Code of Canon Law, XIX-132 pp., 1927.
39. Brown, Mr. Brendan Francis, A.B., LL.M., J.U.D., The Canonical Juristic Personality with Special Reference to its Status in the United States of America, V-212 pp., 1927.

40. CAVANAUGH, REV. WILLIAM THOMAS, C.P., J.U.D., The Reservation of the Blessed Sacrament, VIII-101 pp., 1927.

41. DOHENY, REV. WILLIAM J., C.S.C., A.B., J.U.D., Church Property: Modes of Acquisition, X-118 pp., 1927.

42. FELDHAUS, REV. ALOYSIUS H., C.PP.S., J.C.D., Oratories, IX-141 pp., 1927.

43. KELLY, REV. JAMES PATRICK, A.B., J.C.D., The Jurisdiction of the Simple Confessor, X-208 pp., 1927.

44. NEUBERGER, REV. NICHOLAS J., J.C.D., Canon 6 or the Relation of the Codex Juris Canonici to the Preceding Legislation, V-95 pp., 1927.

45. O'KEEFE, REV. GERALD MICHAEL, J.C.D., Matrimonial Dispensations, Powers of Bishops, Priests, and Confessors, VIII-232 pp., 1927.

46. QUIGLEY, REV. JOSEPH A. M., A.B., J.C.D., Condemned Societies, 139 pp., 1927.

47. ZAPLOTNIK, REV. JOHANNES LEO, J.C.D., De Vicariis Foraneis, X-142 pp., 1927.

48. DUSKIE, REV. JOHN ALOYSIUS, A.B., J.C.D., The Canonical Status of the Orientals in the United States, VIII-196 pp., 1928.

49. HYLAND, REV. FRANCIS EDWARD, J.C.D., Excommunication, Its Nature, Historical Development and Effects, VIII-181 pp., 1928.

50. REINMANN, REV. GERALD JOSEPH, O.M.C., J.C.D., The Third Order Secular of Saint Francis, 201 pp., 1928.

51. SCHENK, REV. FRANCIS J., J.C.D., The Matrimonial Impediments of Mixed Religion and Disparity of Cult, XVI-318 pp., 1929.

52. COADY, REV. JOHN JOSEPH, S.T.D., J.U.D., A.M., The Appointment of Pastors, VIII-150 pp., 1929.

53. KAY, REV. THOMAS HENRY, J.C.D., Competence in Matrimonial Procedure, VIII-164 pp., 1929.

54. TURNER, REV. SIDNEY JOSEPH, C.P., J.U.D., The Vow of Poverty, XLIX-217 pp., 1929.

55. KEARNEY, REV. RAYMOND A., A.B., S.T.D., J.C.D., The Principles of Delegation, VII-149 pp., 1929.

56. CONRAN, REV. EDWARD JAMES, A.B., J.C.D., The Interdict, V-163 pp., 1930.

57. O'NEILL, REV. WILLIAM H., J.C.D., Papal Rescripts of Favor, VII-218 pp., 1930.

58. BASTNAGEL, REV. CLEMENT VINCENT, J.U.D., The Appointment of Parochial Adjutants and Assistants, XV-257 pp., 1930.

59. FERRY, REV. WILLIAM A., A.B., J.C.D., Stole Fees, V-136 pp., 1930.

60. COSTELLO, REV. JOHN MICHAEL, A.B., J.C.D., Domicile and Quasi-Domicile, VII-201 pp., 1930.

61. KREMER, REV. MICHAEL NICHOLAS, A.B., S.T.B., J.C.D., Church Support in the United States, VI-136 pp., 1930.

62. ANGULO, REV. LUIS, C.M., J.C.D., Legislation de la Iglesia sobre la intencion en la application de la Santa Misa, VII-104 pp., 1931.

63. Frey, Rev. Wolfgang Norbert, O.S.B., A.B., J.C.D., The Act of Religious Profession, VIII-174 pp., 1931.
64. Roberts, Rev. James Brendan, A.B., J.C.D., The Banns of Marriage, XIV-140 pp., 1931.
65. Ryder, Rev. Raymond Aloysius, A.B., J.C.D., Simony, IX-151 pp., 1931.
66. Campagna, Rev. Angelo, Ph.D., J.U.D., Il Vicario Generale del Vescovo, VII-205 pp., 1931.
67. Cox, Rev. Joseph Godfrey, A.B., J.C.D., The Administration of Seminaries, VI-124 pp., 1931.
68. Gregory, Rev. Donald J., J.U.D., The Pauline Privilege, XV-165 pp., 1931.
69. Donohue, Rev. John F., J.C.D., The Impediment of Crime, VII-110 pp., 1931.
70. Dooley, Rev. Eugene A., O.M.I., J.C.D., Church Law on Sacred Relics, IX-143 pp., 1931.
71. Orth, Rev. Clement Raymond, O.M.C., J.C.D., The Approbation of Religious Institutes, 171 pp., 1931.
72. Pernicone, Rev. Joseph M., A.B., J.C.D., The Ecclesiastical Prohibition of Books, XII-267 pp., 1932.
73. Clinton, Rev. Connell, A.B., J.C.D., The Paschal Precept, IX-108 pp., 1932.
74. Donnelly, Rev. Francis B., A.M., S.T.L., J.C.D., The Diocesan Synod, VIII-125 pp., 1932.
75. Torrente, Rev. Camilo, C.M.F., J.C.D., Las Procesiones Sagradas, V-145 pp., 1932.
76. Murphy, Rev. Edwin J., C.PP.S., J.C.D., Suspension Ex Informata Conscientia, XI-122 pp., 1932.
77. MacKenzie, Rev. Eric F., A.M., S.T.L., J.C.D., The Delict of Heresy in its Commission, Penalization, Absolution, VII-124 pp., 1932.
78. Lyons, Rev. Avitus E., S.T.B., J.C.D., The Collegiate Tribunal of First Instance, XI-147 pp., 1932.
79. Connolly, Rev. Thomas A., J.C.D., Appeals, XI-195 pp., 1932.
80. Sangmeister, Rev. Joseph V., A.B., J.C.D., Force and Fear as Precluding Matrimonial Consent, V-211 pp., 1932.
81. Jaeger, Rev. Leo A., A.B., J.C.D., The Administration of Vacant and Quasi-Vacant Episcopal Sees in the United States, IX-229 pp., 1932.
82. Rimlinger, Rev. Herbert T., J.C.D., Error Invalidating Matrimonial Consent, VII-79 pp., 1932.
83. Barrett, Rev. John D. M., S.S., J.C.D., A Comparative Study of the Third Plenary Council of Baltimore and the Code, IX-221 pp., 1932.
84. Carberry, Rev. John J., Ph.D., S.T.D., J.C.D., The Juridical Form of Marriage, X-177 pp., 1934.
85. Dolan, Rev. John L., A.B., J.C.D., The Defensor Vinculi, XII-157 pp., 1934.

86. Hannan, Rev. Jerome D., A.M., S.T.D., LL.B., J.C.D., The Canon Law of Wills, IX-517 pp., 1934.
87. Lemieux, Rev. Delise A., A.M., J.C.D., The Sentence in Ecclesiastical Procedure, IX-131 pp., 1934.
88. O'Rourke, Rev. James J., A.B., J.C.D., Parish Registers, VII-109 pp., 1934.
89. Timlin, Rev. Bartholomew, O.F.M., A.M., J.C.D., Conditional Matrimonial Consent, X-381 pp., 1934.
90. Wahl, Rev. Francis X., A.B., J.C.D., The Matrimonial Impediments of Consanguinity and Affinity, VI-125 pp., 1934.
91. White, Rev. Robert J., A.B., LL.B., S.T.B., J.C.D., Canonical Ante-Nuptial Promises and the Civil Law, VI-152 pp., 1934.
92. Herrera, Rev. Antonio Parra, O.C.D., J.C.D., Legislacion Ecclesiastica sobra el Ayuno y la Abstinencia, XI-191 pp., 1935.
93. Kennedy, Rev. Edwin J., J.C.D., The Special Matrimonial Process in Cases of Evident Nullity, X-165 pp., 1935.
94. Manning, Rev. John J., A.B., J.C.D., Presumption of Law in Matrimonial Procedure, XI-111 pp., 1935.
95. Moeder, Rev. John M., J.C.D., The Proper Bishop for Ordination and Dimissorial Letters, VII-135 pp., 1935.
96. O'Mara, Rev. William A., A.B., J.C.D., Canonical Causes for Matrimonial Dispensations, IX-155 pp., 1935.
97. Reilly, Rev. Peter, J.C.D., Residence of Pastors, IX-81 pp., 1935.
98. Smith, Rev. Mariner T., O.P., S.T.Lr., J.C.D., The Penal Law for Religious, VII-169 pp., 1935.
99. Whalen, Rev. Donald W., A.M., J.C.D., The Value of Testimonial Evidence in Matrimonial Procedure, XIII-297 pp., 1935.
100. Cleary, Rev. Joseph F., J.C.D., Canonical Limitations on the Alienation of Church Property, VIII-141 pp., 1936.
101. Glynn, Rev. John C., J.C.D., The Promoter of Justice, XX-337 pp., 1936.
102. Brennan, Rev. James H., S.S., M.A., S.T.B., J.C.D., The Simple Convalidation of Marriage, VI-135 pp., 1937.
103. Brunini, Rev. Joseph Bernard, J.C.D., The Clerical Obligations of Canons 139 and 142, X-121 pp., 1937.
104. Connor, Rev. Maurice, A.B., J.C.D., The Administrative Removal of Pastors, VIII-159 pp., 1937.
105. Guilfoyle, Rev. Merlin Joseph, J.C.D., Custom, XI-144 pp., 1937.
106. Hughes, Rev. James Austin, A.B., A.M., J.C.D., Witnesses in Criminal Trials of Clerics, IX-140 pp., 1937.
107. Jansen, Rev. Raymond J., A.B., S.T.L., J.C.D., Canonical Provisions for Catechetical Instruction, VII-153 pp., 1937.
108. Kealy, Rev. John James, A.B., J.C.D., The Introductory Libellus in Church Court Procedure, XI-121 pp., 1937.

109. McManus, Rev. James Edward, C.SS.R., J.C.D., The Administration of Temporal Goods in Religious Institutes, XVI-196 pp., 1937.

110. Moriarty, Rev. Eugene James, J.C.D., Oaths in Ecclesiastical Courts, X-115 pp., 1937.

111. Rainer, Rev. Eligius George, C.SS.R., J.C.D., Suspension of Clerics, XVII-249 pp., 1937.

112. Reilly, Rev. Thomas F., C.SS.R., J.C.D., Visitation of Religious, VI-195 pp., 1938.

113. Moriarity, Rev. Francis E., C.SS.R., J.C.D., The Extraordinary Absolution from Censures, XV-334 pp., 1938.

114. Connolly, Rev. Nicholas P., J.C.D., The Canonical Erection of Parishes, X-132 pp., 1938.

115. Donovan, Rev. James Joseph, J.C.D., The Pastor's Obligation in Prenuptial Investigation, XII-322 pp., 1938.

116. Harrigan, Rev. Robert J., M.A., S.T.B., J.C.D., The Radical Sanation of Invalid Marriages, VIII-208 pp., 1938.

117. Boffa, Rev. Conrad Humbert, J.C.D., Canonical Provisions for Catholic Schools, VII-211 pp., 1939.

118. Parsons, Rev. Anscar John, O.M.Cap., J.C.D., Canonical Elections, XII-236 pp., 1939.

119. Reilly, Rev. Edward Michael, A.B., J.C.D., The General Norms of Dispensation, XII-156 pp., 1939.

120. Ryan, Rev. Gerald Aloysius, A.B., J.C.D., Principles of Episcopal Jurisdiction, XII-172 pp., 1939.

121. Burton, Rev. Francis James, C.S.C., A.B., J.C.D., A Commentary on Canon 1125, X-222 pp., 1940.

122. Miaskiewicz, Rev. Francis Sigismund, J.C.D., Supplied Jurisdiction According to Canon 209, XII-340 pp., 1940.

123. Rice, Rev. Patrick William, A.B., J.C.D., Proof of Death in Prenuptial Investigation, VIII-156 pp., 1940.

124. Anglin, Rev. Thomas Francis, M.S., J.C.D., The Eucharistic Fast, VIII-183 pp., 1941.

125. Coleman, Rev. John Jerome, J.C.D., The Minister of Confirmation, VI-153 pp., 1941.

126. Downs, Rev. Joseph Emmanuel, A.B., J.C.D., The Concept of Clerical Immunity, XI-163 pp., 1941.

127. Esswein, Rev. Anthony Albert, J.C.D., Extrajudicial Penal Powers of Ecclesiastical Superiors, X-144 pp., 1941.

128. Farrell, Rev. Benjamin Francis, M.A., S.T.L., J.C.D., The Rights and Duties of the Local Ordinary Regarding Congregations of Women Religious of Pontifical Approval, V-195 pp., 1941.

129. Feeney, Rev. Thomas John, A.B., S.T.L., J.C.D., Restitutio in Integrum, VI-169 pp., 1941.

130. Findlay, Rev. Stephen William, O.S.B., A.B., J.C.D., Canonical

Norms Governing the Deposition and Degradation of Clerics, XVII-279 pp., 1941.

131. GOODWINE, REV. JOHN, A.B., S.T.L., J.C.D., The Right of the Church to Acquire Property, VIII-119 pp., 1941.
132. HESTON, REV. EDWARD LOUIS, C.S.C., Ph.D., S.T.D., J.C.D., The Alienation of Church Property in the United States, XII-222 pp., 1941.
133. HOGAN, REV. JAMES JOHN, A.B., S.T.L., J.C.D., Judicial Advocates and Procurators, XIII-200 pp., 1941.
134. KEALY, REV. THOMAS M., A.B., Litt.B., J.C.D., Dowry of Women Religious, IX-152 pp., 1941.
135. KEENE, REV. MICHAEL JAMES, O.S.B., J.C.D., Religious Ordinaries and Canon 198, V-164 pp., 1942.
136. KERIN, REV. CHARLES A., S.S., M.A., S.T.B., J.C.D., The Privation of Christian Burial, XVI-279 pp., 1941.
137. LOUIS, REV. WILLIAM FRANCIS, M.A., J.C.D., Diocesan Archives, X-101 pp., 1941.
138. McDEVITT, REV. GILBERT JOSEPH, A.B., J.C.D., Legitimacy and Legitimation, X-247 pp., 1941.
139. McDONOUGH, REV. THOMAS JOSEPH, A.B., J.C.D., Apostolic Administrators, X-217 pp., 1941.
140. MEIER, REV. CARL ANTHONY, A.B., J.C.D., Penal Administration Procedure Against Negligent Pastors, XI-240 pp., 1941.
141. SCHMIDT, REV. JOHN ROGG, A.B., J.C.D., The Principles of Authentic Interpretation in Canon 17 of the Code of Canon Law, XII-331 pp., 1941.
142. SLAFKOSKY, REV. ANDREW LEONARD, A.B., J.C.D., The Canonical Episcopal Visitation of the Diocese, X-197 pp., 1941.
143. SWOBODA, REV. INNOCENT ROBERT, O.F.M., J.C.D., Ignorance in Relation to the Imputability of Delicts, IX-271 pp., 1941.
144. DUBÉ, REV. ARTHUR JOSEPH, A.B., J.C.D., The General Principles for the Reckoning of Time in Canon Law, VIII-299 pp., 1941.
145. McBRIDE, REV. JAMES T., A.B., J.C.D., Incardination and Excardination of Seculars, XX-585 pp., 1941.
146 KRÓL, REV. JOHN T., J.C.D., The Defendant in Ecclesiastical Trials, XII-207 pp., 1942.
147. COMYNS, REV. JOSEPH J., C.SS.R., A.B., J.C.D., Papal and Episcopal Administration of Church Property, XIV-155 pp., 1942.
148. BARRY, REV. GARRETT FRANCIS, O.M.I., J.C.D., Violation of the Cloister, XII-260 pp., 1942.
149. BOLDUC, REV. GATIEN, C.S.V., A.B., S.T.L., J.C.D., Les Études dans les Religions Cléricales, VIII-155 pp., 1942.
150. BOYLE, REV. DAVID JOHN, M.A., J.C.D., The Juridic Effects of Moral Certitude on Pre-Nuptial Guarantees, XII-188 pp., 1942.
151. CANAVAN, REV. WALTER JOSEPH, M.A., LITT.D., J.C.D., The Profession of Faith, XII-143 pp., 1942.

152. Desrochers, Rev. Bruno, A.B., Ph.L., S.T.B., J.C.D., Le Premier Concile Plénier de Québec et le Code de Droit Canonique, XIV–186 pp., 1942.
153. Dillon, Rev. Robert Edward, A.B., J.C.D., Common Law Marriage, X-148 pp., 1942.
154. Dodwell, Rev. Edward John, Ph.D., S.T.B., J.C.D., The Time and Place for the Celebration of Marriage, X-156 pp., 1942.
155. Donnellan, Rev. Thomas Andrew, A.B., J.C.D., The Obligation of the Misa pro Populo, VII-131 pp., 1942.
156. Eltz, Rev. Louis Anthony, A.B., J.C.L., Cooperation in Crime.
157. Gass, Rev. Sylvester Francis, M.A., J.C.D., Ecclesiastical Pensions, XI-206 pp., 1942.
158. Guiniven, Rev. John Joseph, C.SS.R., J.C.D., The Precept of Hearing Mass, XIV-188 pp., 1942.
159. Gulczynski, Rev. John Theophilus, J.C.D., The Desecration and Violation of Churches, X-126 pp., 1942.
160. Hammill, Rev. John Leo, M.A., J.C.D., The Obligations of the Traveler According to Canon 14, VIII-204 pp., 1942.
161. Haydt, Rev. John Joseph, A.B., J.C.D., Reserved Benefices, XI-148 pp., 1942.
162. Huser, Rev. Roger John, O.F.M., A.B., J.C.D., The Crime of Abortion in Canon Law, XII-187 pp., 1942.
163. Kearney, Rev. Francis Patrick, A.B., S.T.L., J.C.L., The Principles of Canon 1127.
164. Linahen, Rev. Leo James, S.T.L., J.C.D., De Absolutione Complicis In Peccato Turpi, 114 pp., 1942.
165. McCloskey, Rev. Joseph Aloysius, A.B., J.C.D., The Subject of Ecclesiastical Law According to Canon 12, XVII-246 pp., 1942.
166. O'Neill, Rev. Francis Joseph, C.SS.R., J.C.D., The Dismissal of Religious in Temporary Vows, XIII-220 pp., 1942.
167. Prince, Rev. John Edward, A.B., S.T.D., J.C.D., The Diocesan Chancellor, X-136 pp., 1942.
168. Riesner, Rev. Albert Joseph, C.SS.R., J.C.D., Apostates and Fugitives from Religious Institutes, IX-168 pp., 1942.
169. Stenger, Rev. Joseph Bernard, J.C.D., The Mortgaging of Church Property, 186 pp., 1942.
170. Waldron, Rev. Joseph Francis, A.B., J.C.D., The Minister of Baptism, XII-197 pp., 1942.
171. Willett, Rev. Robert Albert, J.C.D., The Probative Value of Documents in Ecclesiastical Trials, X-124 pp., 1942.
172. Woeber, Rev. Edward Martin, M.A., J.C.D., The Interpellations, XII-161 pp., 1942.
173. Benko, Rev. Matthew Aloysius, O.S.B., M.A., J.C.L., The Abbot *Nullius*.

174. CHRIST, REV. JOSEPH JAMES, M.A., S.T.L., J.C.L., Dispensation from Vindictive Penalties.
175. CLANCY, REV. PATRICK M. J., O.P., A.B., S.T.LR., J.C.D., The Local Religious Superior, X-229 pp., 1943.
176. CLARKE, REV. THOMAS JAMES, J.C.D., Parish Societies, XII-147 pp., 1943.
177. CONNOLLY, REV. JOHN PATRICK, S.T.L., J.C.D., Synodal Examiners and Parish Priest Consultors, X-223 pp., 1943.
178. DRUMM, REV. WILLIAM MARTIN, A.B., J.C.L., Hospital Chaplains.
179. FLANAGAN, REV. BERNARD JOSEPH, A.B., S.T.L., J.C.D., The Canonical Erection of Religious Houses, X-147 pp., 1943.
180. KELLEHER, REV. STEPHEN JOSEPH, A.B., S.T.B., J.C.D., Discussions with non-Catholics: Canonical Legislation, X-93 pp., 1943.
181. LEWIS, REV. GORDIAN, C.P., J.C.D., Chapters in Religious Institutes, XII-169 pp., 1943.
182. MARX, REV. ADOLPH, J.C.D., The Declaration of Nullity of Marriages Contracted Outside the Church, X-151 pp., 1943.
183. MATULENAS, REV. RAYMOND ANTHONY, O.S.B., A.B., J.C.L., Communication, a Source of Privileges.
184. O'LEARY, REV. CHARLES GERARD, C.SS.R., J.C.D., Religious Dismissed After Perpetual Profession, X-213 pp., 1943.
185. POWER, REV. CORNELIUS MICHAEL, J.C.L., The Blessing of Cemeteries.
186. SHUHLER, REV. RALPH VINCENT, O.S.A., J.C.D., Privileges of Regulars to Absolve and Dispense, XII-195 pp., 1943.
187. ZIOLKOWSKI, REV. THADDEUS STANISLAUS, A.B., J.C.D., The Consecration and Blessing of Churches, XII-151 pp., 1943.
188. HENEGHAN, REV. JOHN JOSEPH, S.T.D., J.C.L., The Marriages of Unworthy Catholics: Canons 1065 and 1066.
189. CARROLL, REV. COLEMAN FRANCIS, M.A., S.T.L., J.C.L., Charitable Institutions.
190. CIESLUK, REV. JOSEPH EDWARD, Ph.B., S.T.L., J.C.L., National Parishes in the United States.
191. COBURN, REV. VINCENT PAUL, A.B., J.C.L., Marriages of Conscience.
192. CONNORS, REV. CHARLES PAUL, C.S.Sp., A.B., J.C.L., Extra-Judicial Procurators in the Code of Canon Law.
193. COYLE, REV. PAUL RAYMOND, A.B., J.C.L., Judicial Exceptions.
194. FAIR, REV. BARTHOLOMEW FRANCIS, A.B., S.T.L., J.C.L., The Impediment of Abduction.
195. GALLAGHER, REV. THOMAS RAPHAEL, O.P., A.B., S.T.Lr., J.C.L., The Examination of the Qualities of the Ordinand.
196. GANNON, REV. JOHN MARK, S.T.L., J.C.L., The Interstices Required for the Promotion to Orders.
197. GOLDSMITH, REV. J. WILLIAM, B.C.S., S.T.L., J.C.L., The Competence of Church and State over Marriage—Disputed Points.

198. Goodwine, Rev. Joseph Gerard, A.B., S.T.B., J.C.L., The Reception of Converts.
199. Kowalski, Rev. Romuald Eugene, O.F.M., A.B., J.C.L., Sustenance of Religious Houses of Regulars.
200. McCoy, Rev. Alan Edward, O.F.M., J.C.L., Force and Fear in Relation to Delictual Imputability and Penal Responsibility.
201. McDevitt, Rev. Vincent John, Ph.B., S.T.L., J.C.L., Perjury.
202. Martin, Rev. Thomas Owen, Ph.D., S.T.D., J.C.L., Adverse Possession, Prescription and Limitation of Actions: The Canonical "Praescriptio."
203. Miklosovic, Rev. Paul John, A.B., J.C.L., Attempted Marriages and Their Consequent Juridic Effects.
204. Mundy, Rev. Thomas Maurice, A.B., S.T.L., J.C.L., The Union of Parishes.
205. O'Dea, Rev. John Coyle, A.B., J.C.L., The Matrimonial Impediment of Nonage.
206. Olalia, Rev. Alexander Aysón, S.T.L., J.C.L., A Comparative Study of the Christian Constitution of States and the Constitution of the Philippine Commonwealth.
207. Poisson, Rev. Pierre-Marie, C.S.C., A.B., Ph.L., Th.L., J.C.L., Droits Patrimoniaux des Maisons et des Églises Religieuses.
208. Stadalnikas, Rev. Casimir Joseph, M.I.C., J.C.L., Reservation of Censures.
209. Sullivan, Rev. Eugene Henry, S.T.L., J.C.L., Proof of the Reception of the Sacraments.
210. Vaughan, Rev. William Edward, J.C.L., Constitutions for Diocesan Courts.
211. Lyons, Rev. Joseph Henry, J.C.L., The Joinder of Issue in Canonical Trials.

www.ingramcontent.com/pod-product-compliance
Lightning Source LLC
LaVergne TN
LVHW050208080826
844660LV00012B/378

* 9 7 8 0 8 1 3 2 2 3 8 4 1 *